A BIRDWATCHER'S GUIDE TO MOROCCO

PATRICK AND FÉDORA BERGIER

Illustrations by Mike Langman

BIRD WATCHERS' GUIDES

Prion Ltd.
Perry

ACKNOWLEDGEMENTS

We are grateful to all the people who have provided us with information, and especially Dominique Barreau, Jean Paul Julliard, Laurence Lesne and Paul Soto for the ornithological excursions and work we have done together.

A special thanks goes to Pierre Beaubrun and Michel Thèvenot and his family for their warm welcome, the numerous birdwatching trips we had and their close friendship.

Patrick Bergier has been interested in birds since his childhoc and spends most of his free time birdwatching. He and his w Fedora, a holiday tour leader, have visited Morocco a numbe times and have worked there for three years, and have trav through most regions of the country. Patrick has played a lea role in the creation of the 'Centrale Ornithologique Marocaine has published various papers on the birds of Morocco. His about raptors, 'Les Rapaces Diurnes du Maroc', is an imp contribution to Moroccan ornithology.

CONTENTS

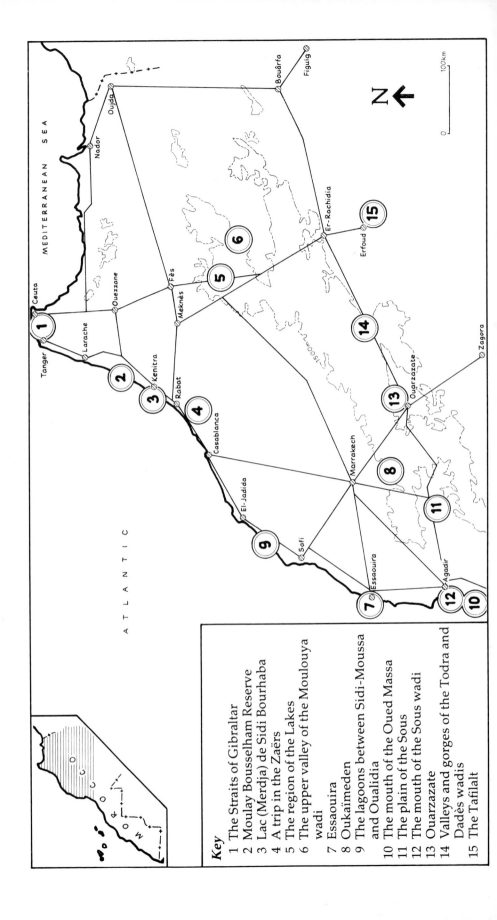

Key

1 The Straits of Gibraltar
2 Moulay Bousselham Reserve
3 Lac (Merdja) de Sidi Bourhaba
4 A trip in the Zaërs
5 The region of the Lakes
6 The upper valley of the Moulouya wadi
7 Essaouira
8 Oukaïmeden
9 The lagoons between Sidi-Moussa and Oualidia
10 The mouth of the Oued Massa
11 The plain of the Sous
12 The mouth of the Sous wadi
13 Ouarzazate
14 Valleys and gorges of the Todra and Dadès wadis
15 The Tafilalt

INTRODUCTION

Morocco is a paradise for birdwatchers with its coasts, islands, wadis, plains, forests, mountains and deserts creating conditions which are often very different from those found in Europe. The richness of these habitats is clearly illustrated by the 414 species which have been recorded north of latitude 28°N, of which 210 are regular breeders.

For the general naturalist there are many attractions other than birds. Minerals from the Middle and High Atlas will interest geologists; palaeontologists will find fossils (the belemnites and goniatites of the Tafilalet are famous); botanists will discover many unfamiliar species, among which are some marvellous orchids, and mammalogists, herpetologists and entomologists will also encounter numerous interesting species. At the end of this Guide there are lists of the birds, mammals, amphibians, reptiles and orchids that have been found in Morocco to date.

Morocco has been inhabited by man since early times as pebble tools and rock carvings show. After prehistoric times several races and cultures developed and mixed: Berbers, a white race whose origins are fairly poorly known but still forms the bulk of the Moroccan population today; Carthaginians; Romans (Volubilis near Meknès, was the first Roman city in Morocco and is well worth visiting). The Arabs invaded the country in the seventh century, bringing a new religion – Islam. Several dynasties followed one another throughout the centuries (Almorhavides, Almohades, Merenides and Saadis) and the Alaouites reign at present. The French Protectorate began on 30 March 1912 and lasted until 1956. Today, the country is governed by H.M. Hassan II, who succeeded his father H.M. Mohammed V in 1961.

Since 1976, Morocco has been at war with the Front Polisario, over the Western Sahara. The whole of Morocco, including Western Sahara, covers 711,000 km (three times the size of Great Britain), but political problems preclude regular access to the southern regions. Consequently no site south of latitude 28°N (south of the Oued Massa) has been described here. The 15 sites which form the main part of this Guide have been chosen for their ornithological importance and also to allow the visiting birdwatcher to experience other aspects of Morocco and its culture.

Red-rumped
Wheatear

PRE-TOUR INFORMATION

A valid passport is needed to enter Morocco. No visa is required for European tourists staying less than 3 months. Other nationalities may be subject to different regulations and should contact their nearest Moroccan Embassy to ascertain the requirements for entry. No inoculations are required to gain entry to the country from Europe. Further information can be obtained from the Moroccan National Tourist Office, 177 Regents Street, LONDON W1 (Tel. (01) 968 00 77).

The Moroccan currency is the dirham (DH) which is divided into 100 centimes. In late 1989 the exchange rate was 13.80 DH to the pound (sterling). Visitors are obliged to declare cash and travellers cheques above 5,000 DH on entry and a receipt is given which will be needed when leaving Morocco. It is strictly prohibited to export dirhams, and only 50 per cent of the initially changed amount of foreign money can be changed back when you leave the country. It is therefore important to keep the exchange receipts given to you, and try to end your trip without too much Moroccan currency. Beware of illicit money changing which offers no receipts and little financial gain.

One of the most comprehensive field guides is the 'Birds of Britain and Europe with the Middle East and North Africa' by Heinzel, Fitter and Parslow. The new 'Birds of the Middle East and North Africa' by Hollom, Porter, Christensen and Willis covers Moroccan specialities in greater detail but needs to be used in conjunction with 'A Field Guide to the Birds of Europe' by Peterson, Mountfort and Hollom. Other books which you may find helpful are listed in the bibliography at the end of this Guide.

Do not use your camera, binoculars and telescope in 'sensitive' areas, e.g. near a military zone. Bring plenty of film. If you run out more may be purchased in tourist areas or in the main cities, but prices are often high. Store your optical equipment in a special bag to keep it free from dust and sheltered from the sun.

One of the best times for birdwatching, from March to June, also corresponds to the busiest tourist period and it is wise to book your flights, car hire and hotels (3 star upwards) well in advance.

Useful addresses in case of emergency are: the British Embassy, 17 Boulevard de la Tour Hassan, BP 45 – RABAT (Tel. (212) 72 09 04 or 31 403) or the British General Consulate, 60 Boulevard d'Anfa, BP 13762 – CASABLANCA (Tel. (212) 22 16 53 or 22 17 41).

Travelling to Morocco

Airports   Morocco has plenty of airports. No less than six cities regularly receive international flights: Tanger, Fès, Rabat, Casablanca, Marrakech and Agadir. If you intend to visit the north of the country it is better to land at Tanger or Casablanca, for visits to the south Agadir is best, while Marrakech occupies a central position for visiting the main birdwatching sites.

All the airports are fairly near the city centres. The maps on the following page give the position of these airports in relation to the cities and the main roads. The farthest away are Tanger and Casablanca, c15 km, but only Nouasser (Casablanca) has a shuttle service to Casablanca (c20 DH) and Rabat (c50 DH). Elsewhere, you will have to take a taxi except at Agadir where there is a city bus stop close by. The airports have all the usual facilities including banks and car hire. Don't forget to reconfirm your return flight at least 72 hours in advance. It is also worth bearing in mind that Moroccan airports do not have duty free shops.

Travelling within Morocco

The most convenient way of touring Morocco is by hiring a car. The driver must be over 25 and have been in possession of a driving licence for at least a year. Most of the large car-hire companies are found in the main cities, but there are also local ones which are often less expensive. Small models such as the Renault 4 are readily available and in 1989 cost 2500–3000 DH for a week (including unlimited mileage and comprehensive insurance). Larger models are also available. Some companies (e.g. InterRent) also offer four-wheel drives, minibuses and Land Rovers with eight seats, driven by a local driver who can act as a guide, interpreter and cook. This last suggestion might be of interest to a group of birdwatchers visiting the country for the first time.

Most of the Moroccan asphalted roads are of good quality. This network, which covers about 30,000 km, is complemented by an equally long network of dirt roads. The quality of the small connecting roads and tracks varies greatly. Some of them, although shown on maps, can be impracticable during certain months of the year, or completely abandoned. Take this into account if you intend to do a long tour off the main roads.

When driving, always bear in mind that anything can happen on Moroccan roads! Watch out for children when driving through villages, and for motor cycles and cattle by the wayside. Try to avoid driving at night as some vehicles have no lights and pedestrians often walk on the roads.

You will find petrol stations all over Morocco, mainly in the towns. In the south, they can be far apart and it is wise to carry a 10 litre stand-by jerry-can. Petrol cost about 6 DH per litre in 1988.

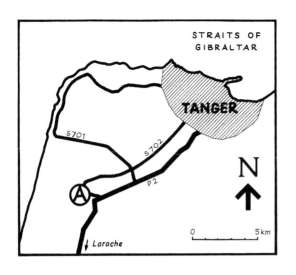

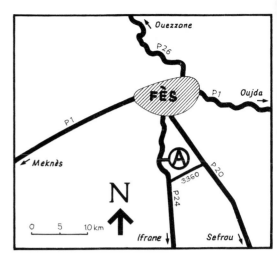

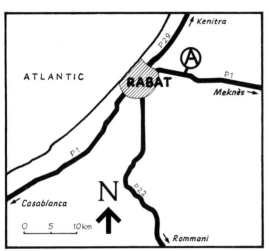

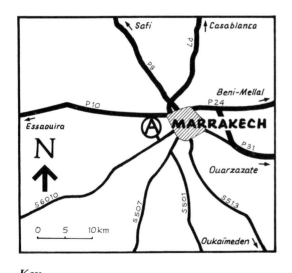

Key

Surfaced roads   Seasonal water   Airport

It is customary, especially in the cities, to give 4 or 5DH to a 'car-keeper' when parking; this will reduce the chance of robbery, but don't leave anything conspicuous inside your car.

A cheap way to travel in Morocco is by coach. Coach lines go everywhere in the whole country; their prices are fixed and attractive, but they are often crowded (especially during the mornings in the south, due to the heat). Unfortunately the timetables are very unreliable. The main coach-line is the C.T.M.L.N. (often called C.T.M., Compagnie des Transports Marocains).

The railway is fairly well developed in the north of the country, with two main lines: Tanger-Rabat-Casablanca-Marrakech and Casablanca-Rabat-Fès-Oujda. The lines to Rabat-Casablanca-Marrakech have recently been improved, and the train is now a very pleasant and cheap way to travel between these cities.

The system of taxis comprises 'small taxis' (individual) and 'large taxis' (collective). Individual taxis only operate inside the towns; they are cheap – even if the price tends to be higher for foreign tourists than for local people. They are numerous, all painted in the same colour in one town and are much more convenient than city buses. If there is no meter in the taxi, ask how much the fare will be before setting off. The 'large taxis', generally big old cars, take up to six persons and are used for trips from one town to another. They leave only when they are fully-booked and it is possible to bargain to get a good price.

Hitch-hiking is not a common practice and a share in expenses may be asked for, however it can be useful in remote areas.

If money is no object there are private airlines such as Air Sud, Ailes Atlas or Royal Air Inter (central reservation tel. 241.44; telex 220.58).

Crested Coot

STAYING IN MOROCCO

Accommodation

Many tourists visit Morocco every year and there is a variety of accommodation to suit all pockets, ranging from 5 star hotels to campsites.

The high standard hotels are concentrated mainly in the larger towns such as Marrakech, Agadir, Tanger, Casablanca, Rabat, Meknès and Fès. Elsewhere, they are few and far between. The country is well equipped with modest hotels (1 or 2 star) and inns. They are usually well kept and prices are attractive (40 to 60 DH per room for two persons) and so they will generally suit birdwatchers as they offer adequate comfort (although it is sometimes necessary to have your own sleeping bag). If you ask they will often prepare you meals.

Morocco also has plenty of campsites, especially by the sea and most of them are pleasant, well situated, cheap and clean. In the non-tourist areas there are very few designated campsites. In these instances it is a good idea to get in touch with the local police, the chief of the village or, failing that, a local person to ask where to camp. Moroccan tea or food will sometimes be offered to you – don't refuse as you may offend (the custom is to offer three glasses of tea). It is also considered polite to give a present when you leave the site.

Food

Moroccan cooking is said to be one of the best in the world with some of the most delicious oriental dishes. The food is spicy but rarely very hot, and comprises such dishes as couscous, tajines, soups, kebabs and pastries. Many different dishes can be found in the numerous restaurants in any town or village.

Couscous is the national dish, combining semolina with a large variety of vegetables cooked with mutton or chicken. Tajines are usually cooked and served in a special round baked-clay dish (called a tajine) and are the equivalent of stews. They can be made with mutton, chicken or fish, with vegetables or almonds, dried plums or olives. Harira is the most popular soup, made with a little meat and lentils – the best ones are often made and sold by women in small village markets. Pastilla is obviously the masterpiece of Moroccan cooking. It is composed of a lot of very thin and crusty pancakes covering a delicious pigeon and almond stuffing. Kebabs are one of the most common dishes. Small restaurants at the main coach stops offer kebabs and glasses of tea but take care to avoid any with chopped meat which may have been reheated. Moroccan pastry is of oriental origin and is based on almond paste, sometimes highly coloured, and honey. It is also found in other Islamic Mediterranean countries. The most famous is called 'corne de gazelle'.

Tea-houses are quite common in the main towns and both oriental and European pastries are normally available. Cafes where you can get soft drinks, beer, coffee and tea are found everywhere throughout the country. A wider variety of alcoholic drinks can only be bought in hotels and in a few stores in main cities.

While on the coast don't miss the opportunity to sample the different types of Moroccan seafood. Try for example the oysters from Oualidia (page 33) or the fish from the Essaouira harbour (page 29).

In addition to typical Moroccan food, you will find international cuisine, largely influenced by the French, mainly in the restaurants of the 3 to 5 star hotels.

Wine is only available in the tourist restaurants and in some stores in the biggest cities. Beer is more common, but Moroccan people generally take water or mineral water (Oulmes, Sidi Harazem, Sidi Ali), soft drinks, coffee and of course the famous tea with mint.

In any town or village, you will find all you need in the grocers, butchers and bakers. Local people prefer to go shopping at the open-air markets, called 'souks', which have a unique atmosphere. Fresh food is only difficult to find in remote areas with low populations.

Banks

Banks are fairly numerous in all the main towns and even in the smaller ones. They generally open from 08.00 to 11.30 and 15.00 to 17.00. During the Ramadan period (an Islamic month of fasting currently in the spring), the duration of opening is shortened, from 09.30 to 14.00. If you are short of money during a weekend, you can exchange currency at the reception desks of main hotels but the rate is usually not as good as at banks.

While travellers cheques (in pounds or, better, in French Francs) and the main international credit cards (American Express, Access/MasterCard/EuroCard and above all Visa) offer a safe way to carry money, their use is less widespread than in Europe. They will be useful only for paying expenses in the main hotels and big souvenir stores, and to get dirhams in the tourist areas, the business districts and the airports. Foreign currency is more easily changed in almost all the banks.

CLIMATE AND CLOTHING

Morocco has been described as 'a cold country where the sunshine is hot'. North of the Sahara, the Moroccan climate is characterized by mild winters, hot summers and generally modest rainfall, concentrated from autumn to spring (especially in November and February–March). As a whole, this climate has been defined as 'Mediterranean' but in fact it varies widely – from the Atlantic ocean to the Algerian border; from the Mediterranean coast to the south of the Atlases, and from sea level to the top of the High Atlas.

The following map shows the distribution of the main bio-climatic areas of Morocco (1: damp, sub-damp and high mountain; 2: semi-arid; 3: arid; 4: Saharan).

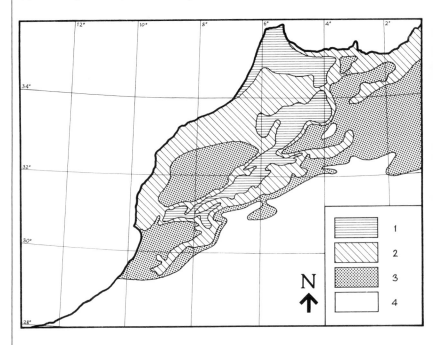

Temperature and rainfall vary widely across the country. The rainfall averages range from 25 mm a year in the Draa valley near Zagora to 2000 mm in the Rif. Temperature differences between summer and winter in a single place can vary by 25–35°C. Moreover, the Moroccan climate varies widely from year to year.

Maximum/minimum temperatures (in degrees Celsius) for a selection of places and months are presented in the following table.

	Jan	March	May	July	Sept	Nov
Tanger	15/10	17/11	21/14	26/19	25/18	19/13
Casablanca	17/8	20/10	22/14	26/19	26/18	21/12
Ifrane	9/–4	13/0	18/5	31/12	25/9	14/1
Marrakech	18/5	23/9	29/14	38/20	33/18	23/10
Agadir	20/7	23/11	24/14	26/18	27/17	24/12
Zagora	21/3	26/10	23/19	44/27	36/21	26/11

The most suitable clothing will depend upon the time of year and location. Generally casual clothes and good shoes for walking will suffice. Neutral colours are more suitable than bright ones when birdwatching. In summer, avoid synthetic materials and choose linen or cotton. Don't forget a hat, a swimsuit and sunglasses. Even during the hot months, bring a pullover for the evenings and, if you intend to take a trip in the mountains, a warm anorak. From late autumn to spring, take warm clothes and a waterproof jacket.

HEALTH AND MEDICAL FACILITIES

There is very little chance of catching a serious disease in Morocco. However, some precautions should be taken to ensure a pleasant stay. Firstly you should of course be up to date with all standard vaccinations. Although no specific inoculations are required on entry it is wise to be immunized against cholera, typhoid, polio and tetanus.

The most frequent problem that European tourists encounter in Morocco is gastro-enteritis. Although often mild it can still be a great nuisance. It is difficult to avoid as it is often due to a change in diet. Following some simple rules will help to prevent a bad attack. Eat well-cooked meat; wash vegetables and fruits; don't drink too much fruit juice and try to drink only bottled drinks and boiled or mineral water, especially outside the main towns. If you intend to spend a long period outside towns or tourist sites, it is a good idea to take tablets for water sterilisation. Common gastro-enteritis can be cured by tablets such as Imodium and Ercefuryl (available in Moroccan pharmacies). With severe or persistent symptoms a local doctor should be consulted.

If you should sustain dog or snake bites (fortunately extremely rare) you should be treated by a doctor as quickly as possible. Anti-snake bite serums are available, but they are difficult and inconvenient to keep.

There is no fatal scorpion in northern Morocco, but their bites can sometimes be painful and give some trouble; don't hesitate to take medical advice. In the south, avoid walking barefoot in the marshes and bathing in the wadis because of bilharziosis.

Lastly, be careful to avoid sunburn. Bring adequate clothes (especially some long-sleeved shirts), sunglasses and protective cream. A mosquito repellant will also be useful.

Every main town has good hospitals and clinics and there are also numerous doctors (general practitioners and specialists) and pharmacies. In villages and small towns, medical facilities are not as widespread and often only a dispensary exists. Be sure to check that your travel insurance covers medical costs, including repatriation in case of severe disease or accident.

MAPS

Since the acquisition of the new Saharan Provinces, Morocco stretches as far south as 21°N. As this boundary is still in dispute, few maps show the entire country. People visiting Morocco may encounter problems at customs when carrying maps which don't include Western Sahara.

Several publishers have produced maps, which are generally excellent:

Morocco, scale 1:800,000 (Roger Lascelles).
Maroc, scale 1:800,000 (Astrolabe).
Morocco, scale 1:900,000 (Hildebrand's Travel Map).
Morocco, scale 1:1,000,000 (Kümmerly + Frey).
Maroc, scale 1:1,400,000 (Marcus, Paris)
The first and last of these are perhaps the best.

Michelin publishes a small-scale map which shows Morocco in a wider context – 'Africa – Nord et Ouest', no. 153 (953), scale 1:4,000,000, and used to publish an excellent map of Morocco (no. 169), scale 1:1,000,000 which may be reprinted in the near future as no. 969.

Most of these maps are available from Stanfords International Map Centre, 12–14 Long Acre, Covent Garden, London WC2E 9LP and from Astrolabe, 46 Rue de Provence, 75009 Paris.

In Morocco only one map is commonly found, scale 1:1,850,000, edited by Carima. Two others are rarer: Maroc, scale 1:2,500,000 (Imprimerie principale) and the Marcus' map. The small scale of these maps makes them less useful.

An excellent series of maps (scales 1:100,000 and 1:50,000) which are most useful for birdwatchers are produced by a branch of the 'Ministère de l'Agriculture et de la Réforme agraire', called 'Division de la Cartographie' (31 Avenue Moulay Hassan, Rabat). If you intend to make a long stay, undertake a detailed study in a special area, or take a trip off the main roads, we recommend you stop at Rabat in order to buy the relevant maps. A few of these are available from Stanfords.

In the northern half of Morocco, between 28°N and 36°N and 1°W and 12°W, the biological seasons are the same as in western Europe.

From an ornithological point of view, the period from March to May is probably the most interesting as a wide variety of species, migrants as well as residents, are present. This is the most pleasant time of the year as after the winter and early spring rains the weather is generally mild and the sun shines most of the time.

Among the most conspicuous migrants are the raptors and the waders. Most of the Lesser Kestrels pass through in March, Black Kites, Egyptian Vultures, Short-toed Eagles and Hen Harriers in March-April and Honey Buzzards in April. Ospreys, Booted Eagles and Hobbies pass through anytime from March to May and the migration of Montagu's Harriers begins at the end of March and goes on until the beginning of May.

Most waders such as Black-winged Stilts, Grey Plovers, Knots, Sanderlings, Little Stints, Curlew Sandpipers, Dunlins, Ruffs, Curlews, Greenshanks and Wood and Common Sandpipers migrate from March to May. Green Sandpipers are mainly seen from mid-March to mid-April. The first Collared Pratincoles arrive in mid-March.

On the Atlantic coast, most species of gulls and terns migrate througout the spring. Audouin's Gull moves from February to mid-April, Black Tern from late March to the beginning of May and Whiskered and White-winged Black Terns from the beginning of March to the beginning of May.

Of the migrants which breed in Morocco, Red-rumped Swallows, Tawny Pipits, Desert Wheatears, Subalpine and Bonelli's Warblers and Woodchat Shrikes arrive in early March. From mid-March Bee-eaters, Short-toed Larks, Nightingales, Wheatears (Moroccan race), Black-eared Wheatears and Spectacled and Orphean Warblers can be seen. Blue-cheeked Bee-eaters, Rollers, and Olivaceous Warblers begin to appear from late March. From the beginning of April Rufous Bush Robins, Melodious Warblers, Spotted Flycatchers and Golden Orioles arrive.

In the plains north of the Atlas Mountains, breeding generally begins in March and goes on until June. In semi-desert and desert areas, the season is approximately the same. Early nests have been found in January (e.g. Hoopoe Lark) during favourable (wet) years although even then laying can occur very late. Sandgrouse seem to breed mainly in June, when the weather is becoming very hot.

In June the climate begins to become uncomfortably hot, except near the coast or in the mountains. At Oukaimeden for example (site 8), breeding is in full swing (Shorelarks, Tawny Pipits, Black and Moussier's Redstarts, Wheatears and Rock Sparrows).

In July and August, the heat may be unbearable away from the coast and the high mountains. Breeding is over, and some species have already begun their autumn migration by August (e.g. Honey Buzzards, Black Kites, Egyptian Vultures, Montagu's Harriers and Booted Eagles).

In September many species begin their migration and the first wintering birds are generally noted from the end of this month, or in October. During this period, the best sites to visit are located on the Atlantic coast but a visit in the Straits area (page 15), to observe the unforgettable raptor migration is well worthwhile.

In November, most of the wintering birds have arrived in the country. This month is generally one of the wettest of the year and all the wetlands along the Atlantic coast are worth visiting. With a little luck, some rarities will be discovered among the more common birds.

Even though the temperatures are decreasing, December and January are generally more agreeable, with less humidity and more sunshine. Christmas and New Year are particularly pleasant along the southern Atlantic coast. If you intend to take a trip at this time, try to spend several days at Massa (page 35). Besides the thousands of coots and ducks, you should see the first spring migrants of such species as Great Spotted Cuckoo, Hoopoe, Pallid Swift, Swallow and Red-rumped Swallow.

In the semi-desert and desert areas, the nights are fairly cold (water can freeze in the palm-groves) but the days are generally pleasant. Seize the opportunity to visit such sites as the Ouarzazate Barrage and the Draa valley (page 42) or the Tafilalet (page 47), with the famous daya of Merzouga – a temporary lake in the open desert, which attracts hundreds, sometimes thousands, of birds during wet years.

During this period mountains are covered with snow, and several roads and passes are blocked. Birdwatching becomes difficult there, except in places such as the Ifrane region (page 24) or Oukaimeden (page 31), two spots where skiing resorts have been built.

In January and the beginning of February the largest concentrations of White Storks may be seen. Several hundred birds often gather (e.g. 700 on 5 February 1981, on the refuse dump of Marrakech city). In February the rains begin again, and allow the vegetation to grow. The spring migration intensifies and by the end of the month the first breeding begins.

Throughout the year a birdwatcher will always find something interesting in Morocco, whether in the plains, wetlands, mountains or deserts. Always bear in mind that some places are better than others, depending on the time of year.

African Marsh Owl

INTRODUCTION TO THE SITE INFORMATION

The places described include not only specific sites such as the mouths of the Sous and Massa rivers, the lake of Sidi Bourhaba and the biological reserve of Moulay Bousselham, but also wider areas. Generally, these areas contain smaller densities of birds and they have been included because of their important ecological interest. The foreign birdwatcher can become familiar with the typical Moroccan fauna and flora by visiting these habitats: desert and oases (Tafilalet); semi-desert steppes with alfa-grass (upper valley of the Moulouya wadi); the cork-oak and Sandarac woods (Zaërs); the cedar-woods and lakes of the Middle Atlas (the region of the lakes); the valleys and mountains of the High Atlas (Oukaïmeden and the valleys and gorges of Todra and Dades rivers); the Argana forest (Souss); the Juniper woods (Essaouira).

The sections on birds do not list all of the species that have been recorded at these sites, but try to emphasize the species that may be of interest to European birdwatchers. A complete list of all the birds seen in Morocco is included at the end of the Guide.

The maps of the larger areas only show the main roads and tracks. To obtain more information on these areas, you should buy the large scale maps described on page 10. Bear in mind that the condition of the roads and tracks can change quickly from one year to another and sometimes from one hour to another!

This is one of the best places in the world to observe migration. Only 15 kilometres separate Africa from Europe, and the spectacular movement of migrants should not be missed. More than 250 species, mainly European, have been noted in the Straits. Most follow a NE-SW axis and some are much more conspicuous than others. The raptors are the most spectacular, but the migration of shearwaters, storks, flamingos, gulls, bee-eaters, larks, swallows, wagtails and finches can also be quite impressive.

Location

The close proximity of Tanger makes it the ideal base for exploring the Straits. As one of Morocco's busiest ports it is very well served by sea, air, railway or road. If coming from Spain, you can cross the Straits to Ceuta (the shortest crossing) and then enter Morocco.

Key

Surfaced roads

Marsh

International frontier

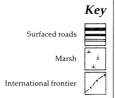

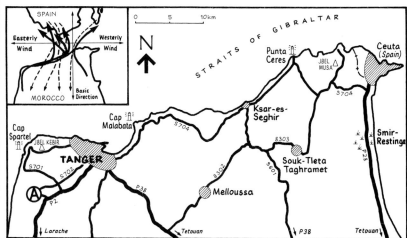

Accommodation

It is not difficult to find accommodation in Tanger. The list of recommended places below is far from comprehensive but includes a selection to suit all tastes. The least expensive hotels are situated in the medina, near Petit Socco square (try the Pension Fuentes or Pension Nahda). The more expensive hotels include the Hotel Valencia (two star (A), 72 av. des F.A.R., close to the harbour), the Shéhérazade (three star (A), 11 av. des F.A.R.), the Villa de France (four star (B), 143 rue de Hollande) or one of the few five star hotels. The Miramonte camping site is at the west end of the city, the Timgis site at the east. The city of Tetouan, in the SE of the peninsula, is also well served by hotels.

There are many restaurants in Tanger providing a wide variety of food. Some of the least expensive ones can be found around Petit Socco square (the Ahlen or Le Moderne). Most of the three, four and five star hotels have their own restaurants.

Strategy

Migrants pass through the Tanger peninsula during most months of the year and occasionally the last of the autumn migrants and the first of the spring may be seen together (for example storks or swallows). The most important movements occur from March to May and August to October.

Visible migration takes place in the morning and the afternoon. Most activity begins about two hours after sunrise and continues into the afternoon. The important visible passages generally stop between one and three hours before sunset. The route of the migrants varies according to climatic conditions. As a general rule, the movements take place in the east of the peninsula when winds come from the west (mainly in spring and November), and in the west when winds blow from the east (mainly in September-October).

The spring movement of raptors varies according to the wind conditions as follows. With strong winds from the east, the migrants are noted on the western coast of the peninsula, from Larache and particularly near Cap Spartel, where their densities increase with the wind. They then follow the southern side of the Straits eastwards and leave Africa between Ksar-es-Seghir and Jbel Musa. The stronger the wind, the lower they fly. With westerly winds, they travel mainly along the east of the peninsula, following the southern side of the Straits westwards and leaving at Punta Ceres (see map insert, page 15). With gentle winds, birds leave from the entire eastern third of the peninsula and when the wind is very weak, birds leave from everywhere, often at very high altitude. Hundreds of raptors such as kites, harriers and falcons, gather to roost in the scrub of Jbel Kebir or in the forest at the west of Tanger.

In autumn, with westerly winds, most raptors reach Morocco near Punta Ceres (the favoured arrival point, being closest to Spain and creating good thermals). On the other hand, easterly winds spread them west of Punta Ceres and they can even miss the southern side of the Straits.

If time allows, look at the wetlands of Smir-Restinga, on the P28 which is good for ducks, particularly Red-crested Pochard. Glossy Ibis and Slender-billed Curlew have been seen there in winter. Audouin's Gull is often seen on the beaches south of Smir-Restinga, from August to April.

Birds   The table shows the migration periods of the commonest raptors which cross the Straits and the estimate of their numbers in autumn (after Pineau and Giraud–Audine 1979). Almost all the species follow the general pattern that has been described, but there are some exceptions. Harriers, accipiters, Ospreys and falcons are less concentrated by the Straits and move on a broader front. Short-toed Eagles are rarely noted at Cap Spartel, Booted Eagles are rare in the west of the peninsula and Lesser Kestrels are mainly seen in spring. Storks behave in the same way as raptors.

Large numbers of shearwaters move through the Straits. Cory's are noted from mid-February to early May and late August to late November. Two races of Manx (which may be separate species) pass through at different times: Balearic Shearwaters are present from December to mid-April and late August to October; Yelkouan Shearwaters are mainly seen between late June and September.

The passage of Bee-eaters, swifts and passerines is light, except in spring when there are strong easterly winds, and they are frequently observed in huge numbers near Cap Spartel.

Several eastern migrants have been seen, far from their normal routes, mainly in spring. These include Pallid Harrier, Spotted Eagle, Red-footed Falcon, Great Snipe, Marsh Sandpiper, White-winged Black Tern, Richard's Pipit, Red-breasted Flycatcher and Red-backed Shrike.

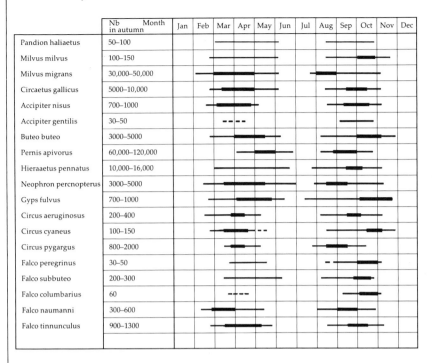

	Nb Month in autumn	Jan	Feb	Mar	Apr	May	Jun	Jul	Aug	Sep	Oct	Nov	Dec
Pandion haliaetus	50–100												
Milvus milvus	100–150												
Milvus migrans	30,000–50,000												
Circaetus gallicus	5000–10,000												
Accipiter nisus	700–1000												
Accipiter gentilis	30–50												
Buteo buteo	3000–5000												
Pernis apivorus	60,000–120,000												
Hieraaetus pennatus	10,000–16,000												
Neophron percnopterus	3000–5000												
Gyps fulvus	700–1000												
Circus aeruginosus	200–400												
Circus cyaneus	100–150												
Circus pygargus	800–2000												
Falco peregrinus	30–50												
Falco subbuteo	200–300												
Falco columbarius	60												
Falco naumanni	300–600												
Falco tinnunculus	900–1300												

Other wildlife

The Straits are an exceptional area to observe cetaceans especially from boats. The commonest are Bottlenose and Common Dolphins and Long-finned Pilot Whale.

Moulay Bousselham Reserve The Merdja Zerga

This internationally important wetland was declared a biological reserve in 1978. Covering 90 sq km, it includes one of the largest lagoons in Morocco (the Merdja Zerga, 30 sq km).

The lagoon, surrounded by a wide belt of low vegetation, is an important staging and wintering place for ducks and waders, and a breeding site for some uncommon birds. It also acts as a sanctuary when climatic conditions are unfavourable in Europe, especially in southern Spain.

Location

This wetland is located on the Atlantic coast, 40 km south of Larache and 70 km north of Kénitra. The quickest way to get there by car is to drive along the main road (P2) to Souk el Arba du Rharb, then go west to the site along the S216A (c.40 km to the village of Moulay Bousselham). A nicer route which can be taken from the south follows the S206 from Kénitra for 25 km and then the 2301 that runs along the Atlantic coast.

C.T.M. buses stop at Souk el Arba, which is an important cross-roads. From there you should have no difficulty in hitch-hiking or in taking another bus to the site.

Key

Surfaced roads

Unsurfaced roads/tracks

Marsh

Sand

Open water (permanent)

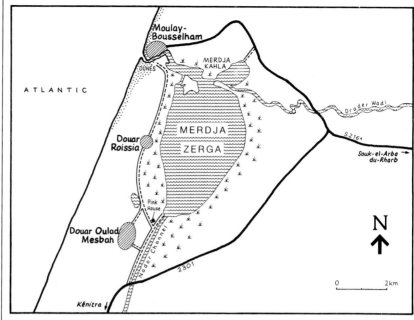

Accommodation

The village of Moulay Bousselham has a hotel ('Le Lagon', three star) but it is often fully booked at weekends. There is a nice campsite 500 metres before entering the village, and some restaurants nearby. Those camping may like to buy the fresh fish which are available when the fishermen come back in the afternoon.

Strategy

Because of the wealth of birdlife at the site, it is worth spending a couple of days there.

Winter is the season when birds are most numerous and it is possible to see more than 1,000 Greater Flamingos, 30,000 ducks, 40,000 Coots and 50,000 waders. Visits to the site can be rewarding in spring and autumn, when a lot of passage migrants stop there and breeding birds are present. Try to avoid the middle of hot days because of the heat haze.

The Merdja Kahla is easily reached by walking from Moulay Bousselham. It is an excellent spot to observe most species and best visited early in the morning.

At Moulay Bousselham, you can ask a fisherman to take you across the narrow channel in front of the village and bring you back some hours later; you will then have access to the wild western bank of the lagoon which you should follow to the south.

If you have a car at your disposal, travel round the lagoon on the 2301. The road runs quite near the lagoon giving good views. During the breeding season you can see White Storks at close range at their nests, built on the low huts of the villages. When you arrive at the south of the lagoon, where the road crosses the Nador Channel, there is a track that hugs the western bank. This track leads to the southern edge of the lagoon and is only suitable for vehicles in the dry period. It is watched over by wardens and it is imperative to stay on the track as you are in the reserve, do not go walking elsewhere.

Birds

Half of all the ducks and the small waders wintering in Morocco north of latitude 30°N are found at the Merdja Zerga. Among the ducks, Wigeon is the commonest (c.20,000, 90% of the population wintering in the country), followed by Mallard and Shoveler (c.2,000 each), Shelduck and Teal. The rarest are probably Ruddy Shelduck and Marbled, Ferruginous and Tufted Ducks. Of the waders, the most abundant are Dunlin (c.20,000), Black-tailed Godwit (c.10,000), Ringed Plover (c.5,000), Redshank (c.3,000), Avocet and Kentish Plover (c.2,000 each), and Snipe. In recent winters very small numbers of Slender-billed Curlews have been found at this site. If you see any of this very rare species be careful not to disturb them and report your sightings to the International Council for Bird Preservation, 32 Cambridge Road, Girton, Cambridge, CB3 0PJ, Great Britain. Little Egrets, Grey Herons, White Storks and geese (mainly Greylag) are also present.

1,500–2,500 Greater Flamingos and 10–40 Spoonbills winter here; their numbers increase during the migration periods in September–October and especially in March–April; in April 1982 up to 6,700 Greater Flamingos and 115 Spoonbills were counted.

The total number of birds present at the lagoon is smaller in spring and autumn, but there is a greater variety. From early March to mid-May and from late August to late November, the majority of the Western Palearctic migrant waders and a lot of migrant passerines are likely to be seen.

During the breeding season (March–June), the area around the lagoon supports a good number of species. Turtle Doves, Crested Larks, Yellow Wagtails, Fan-tailed Warblers and Corn Buntings are abundant. Black Kites, Marsh and Montagu's Harriers and Ospreys (1–5 non-breeding birds present throughout the year) should be seen. At the south of the lagoon more than 1000 pairs of Collared Pratincoles nest as well as the most southern breeding colony of Lapwing. This is one of the best sites to see African Marsh Owl and Red-necked Nightjar and both are best watched for near sunset. The owl can be seen around the lagoon while the nightjar can be found in the cork oak forest nearby.

Slender-billed Curlew

Of the gulls and terns, only Little Terns breed (c.25 pairs), but many other species winter or pass through. Mediterranean Gulls have been noted amongst the commoner wintering species. Spring is the season when the majority of the other species have been observed: Slender-billed and Audouin's Gulls, and Gull-billed, Royal, Lesser Crested, Whiskered and Black Terns. Caspian Terns can be seen throughout the year.

Some rare species for Morocco or for the Western Palaearctic have been noted here: Great White Egret, Lesser Flamingo, Mute Swan, Allen's Gallinule and Ring-billed Gull.

Other wildlife   Several species of amphibians and reptiles can be observed around the lagoon among which are Sharp-ribbed Salamander, Moroccan Toad, Spiny-footed Lizard and Montpellier and Viperine Snakes.

Lac (Merdja) de Sidi Bourhaba

This nice lagoon, surrounded by juniper woodland, runs parallel to the Atlantic coast between two rows of consolidated dunes. Its southern half, a biological reserve since 1976 with prohibited access, is part open water and part marsh, and its banks are densely wooded. The northern half, freely accessible, forms a lake fringed by a small marsh. It shelters several hundred wintering ducks and is a breeding place for various interesting species.

Location   Sidi Bourhaba is located 30 km north of Rabat, west of the P2, near Kénitra and the village of Mehdiya. The best way to get there is to hire a car in Rabat or alternatively take the Kénitra bus and ask the driver to stop at the junction of the S212, the road to Sidi Bourhaba. A colony of Cattle Egrets breeds here in certain years. From the junction you can then hitch-hike to the lagoon.

Accommodation   There is no accommodation or shops, and camping is not recommended by the lake itself. A camping site is open in summer near the Sebou Wadi and other accommodation is available in Rabat or Kénitra. It is pleasant to bring a picnic and have lunch near the lagoon; tables and benches have been built under the eucalyptus on the eastern bank.

Strategy   You can visit the site throughout the year, but summer is rather quiet and the birds are less numerous and more difficult to see. Ducks are abundant throughout the winter, and a visit in March will enable you to see some migrants and the first breeding birds as well.

It is a good idea to spend a day at the site, but avoid Sundays, when people from Kénitra and Rabat visit in great numbers. Try to stay until sunset, when you may see African Marsh Owl.

The road which overlooks the lagoon provides a good viewpoint and you can walk everywhere, except in the reserve. The western edges are best, especially the small marsh at the northern tip. At low tide, it is worth visiting the fishing harbour on the Sebou Wadi for waders, gulls and terns – Royal Tern has been seen here.

Key

Surfaced roads	
Marsh	
Open water (permanent)	
Shrine	
Camping	

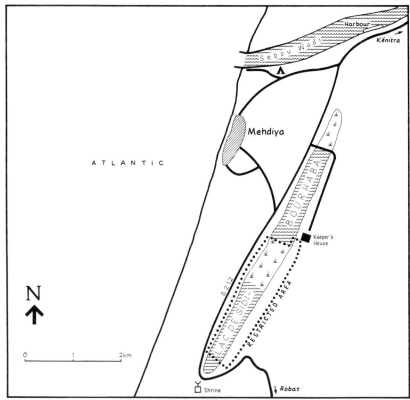

Birds

In winter, mixed with the flocks of European ducks (c.3,000–4,000), you may see Marbled Ducks (up to 1,700 in January 1982). Waders and herons can be seen along the banks and the woods harbour numerous wintering passerines. At this time, Crested Coots (c.20 pairs) are harder to distinguish from Coots but from February or March, as the breeding season starts, their red knobs appear. Great Crested Grebes (c.10 pairs) and Marsh Harriers begin to display and, at dusk African Marsh Owls can be seen hunting over the marsh by the north-west tip of the restricted area and sometimes from the causeway at the north end of the lagoon.

Migration is at its peak in April, and involves such species as Squacco and Purple Herons, Greater Flamingos, Montagu's Harriers and Avocets. In May and June, sometimes sooner, breeding Black-winged Stilts and families of Marbled Ducks and coots can be seen. A lot of passerines breed around the lagoon and Cetti's, Fan-tailed and Sardinian Warblers are fairly common. A colony of the Moroccan race of Magpie, with a blue patch behind the eye, breeds in the reserve, and Hobbies often come to hunt over the water.

Some rare species for Morocco and the Western Palearctic have been noted here: Fulvous Whistling Duck, Blue-winged Teal, Ring-necked Duck and Sabine's Gull.

Other wildlife

The woodland around the lagoon shelters several reptiles including Mediterranean Chameleon, Spiny-footed Lizard and Horseshoe Snake. The Spur-thighed Tortoise is common.

A trip in the Zaërs

The Zaërs form the western part of the Central Moroccan Plateau and contain some of the original cork-oak and Sandarac woods. Their rich avifauna (c.100 breeding species) includes some rare species such as Black-shouldered Kite, Double-spurred Francolin and Black-headed Bush Shrike.

Location

The most interesting part of this region, and the easiest to visit, is located in the Rabat-Casablanca-Rommani triangle. A car is needed to fully explore this area.

Accommodation

Rabat and Casablanca have numerous hotels, of all types. Camp-sites can be found at Casablanca or Mohammedia, or, better still the one at Ben Slimane, under the cork-oaks.

Strategy

One of the best times to visit the region is early spring, in March or April. A lot of migrants such as Bee-eater, Rufous Bush Robin and Olivaceous Warbler arrive from April onwards and leave in September–October. After a rainy winter, there are hundreds of dayas (temporary ponds), an abundance of flowers and the lush green forests resound with birdsong. Migrants should be plentiful.

Key

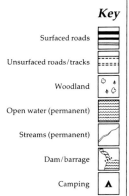

Surfaced roads

Unsurfaced roads/tracks

Woodland

Open water (permanent)

Streams (permanent)

Dam/barrage

Camping

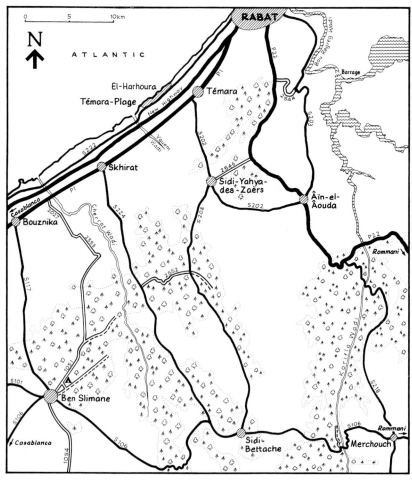

Double-spurred
Francolin

One day is sufficient to cover the region but if time allows a longer stay can be worthwhile. If based at Rabat, a suitable one-day itinerary is as follows: Rabat – Aïn el Aouda – Merchouch (P22/S218) – Sidi Bettache (S106) – Sidi Yahya des Zaërs (S208) – Témara (S202) – Rabat (P1). Start early in the morning as there is plenty to see and the day soon passes. Explore some of the numerous tracks which go deep into the forests and down into the valleys.

If you stay several days, visit the coast, the famous cork-oak woods of Mamora to the north-east of Rabat, and take the opportunity to go to the Lac de Sidi Bourhaba (see page 20).

Birds

One of the main features of the region is the numerous breeding passerines. In the fields and cultivated areas there are Calandra and Thekla Larks, Stonechats, Fan-tailed Warblers, Great Grey Shrikes, Spanish Sparrows and Cirl and Corn Buntings. Rufous Bush Robins, Nightingales and abundant Sardinian Warblers live in the bushes while Common Bulbuls and Cetti's and Olivaceous Warblers are attracted by the vegetation that fringes the wadis. Spotted Flycatchers, Blue (Moroccan race) and Great Tits, Short-toed Treecreepers, Golden Orioles, Woodchat Shrikes, Black-headed Bush Shrikes and Jays prefer the forests.

Cattle Egrets and White Storks are numerous and some Barbary Partridges may be seen. This is the best place in Morocco to see Double-spurred Francolin which inhabits the undergrowth of the cork-oak woods near Sidi Bettache and Ben Slimane. The forest along the S208 between Sidi Bettache and Sidi Yahya is perhaps the best area to look for this bird which is particularly vocal in the early morning.

Raptors are fairly common. Black-shouldered and Black Kites, Short-toed Eagles, Marsh and Montagu's Harriers, Sparrowhawks, Long-legged Buzzards, Golden, Booted and Bonelli's Eagles, Lesser Kestrels, Kestrels, Hobbies and Lanners all breed here.

The wadis and their surroundings attract Little Ringed Plovers, Kingfishers, Bee-eaters and Red-rumped Swallows.

The birds along the coast include Collared Pratincoles, Kentish Plovers (resident) and Little Terns which breed on the beach near Skhirat. Collared Pratincoles sometimes breed in the inland fields. Large numbers of Pallid Swifts gather over the city walls of Rabat at dusk.

A wide range of waders and gulls stop along the shore. A glance at the mouth of the Yquem wadi is often interesting. Mediterranean and Audouin's Gulls and Royal and Lesser Crested Terns have been reported, mainly in spring, summer and autumn.

Among the species that pass through the region in good numbers are Great Spotted Cuckoo (Jan-Feb), Black Kite (March-April) and Bee-eater (April-May). A large number of European passerines come to spend the winter, as do Marsh Harriers whose roosts can contain more than 70 birds.

Other wildlife

Several species of amphibians and reptiles live in this region and Horseshoe Snake and Moroccan Toad are of particular interest. From February to April orchids are in flower: Yellow Bee, Moroccan Bee, Mirror, Sawfly and Moroccan Woodcock Ophrys, Green-winged, Milky and Naked Man Orchids, Long-lipped and Heart-flowered Tongue Orchids.

The region of the Lakes

This area to the north-east of the Middle Atlas contains a cross-section of interesting habitats such as the cedar woods, the stony plateaux ('causses') and the lakes (called 'dayèts'). Several endemic subspecies and species and some Moroccan rarities can be found here.

Location

The region is located some 50 km south of Fès. The city (and skiing resort) of Ifrane, a good starting point for trips, can be easily reached by bus.

Accommodation

Ifrane is probably the best base with plenty of hotels: the five star Michliffen, the three star (A) Grand Hotel and the three star (B) Perce Neige. An alternative base is the charming little town of Azrou, although it is situated 17 km to the south-west of Ifrane. Hotels here include the two star (A) Panorama, the one star (A) Des Cèdres and the one star (A) Azrou. Other alternatives include the inn near Dayèt Âaoua, or the camp site at Ifrane.

Strategy

The north-east Middle Atlas is generally under snow from late December to February making the tracks and sometimes the roads impassable. Birdwatching is not very interesting at this time but you can go skiing at Ifrane. The best period for birds is from April to July. August and September are quieter months but a visit can be made to escape the heat of the surrounding plains.

The region can be explored by car in a couple of days. Most of the tracks are drivable but are poorly marked, however there is little risk of getting lost. An interesting circuit consists of visiting the five main lakes Dayèts Hachlaf, Ifrah, Iffer, Afourgah and Âaoua (see map), stopping to explore the various habitats en route. If you have more time to spare then walking and camping is a good way to see the wildlife.

To the north-west of Ifrane the road to El-Hajeb (S309) passes through the forest of Jabaa (beautiful oak woodland, good for birds). In El-Hajeb itself be sure to see the colony of Lesser Kestrels in the old walls.

To the south of Ifrane the lake of Aguelmane Aziga, above Khénifra, is worth visiting for the splendid scenery. If travelling on to the upper valley of the Moulouya Wadi (site 6) stop at Foum Kheneg gorge on the P21 south of Timahdite, and Aguelmane Sidi Ali near the Zad pass, for the abundant Ruddy Shelducks.

Birds

The Dayèts Hachlaf, Afourgah and Âaoua are probably the most interesting of the five main lakes. In May and June you can see or hear Little Bittern, Marsh Harrier, Coot, Crested Coot, Black-winged Stilt and Savi's and Great Reed Warblers. Dayèt Afourgah has a colony of herons in some years: Night Heron, Cattle and Little Egrets and perhaps Purple Heron.

Key

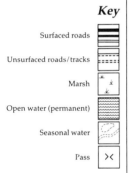

Surfaced roads

Unsurfaced roads/tracks

Marsh

Open water (permanent)

Seasonal water

Pass

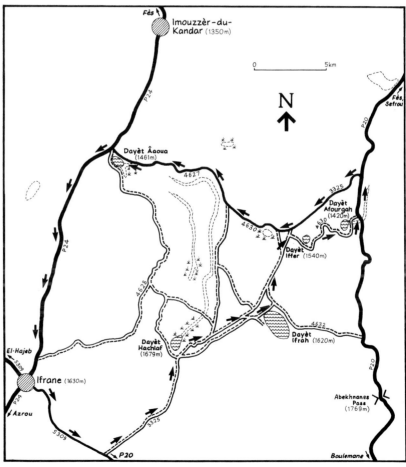

Numerous passerines breed in the cedar and holm-oak woods and include endemic subspecies of Mistle Thrush, Firecrest, Pied Flycatcher, Coal Tit, Blue Tit, Great Tit, Nuthatch, Short-toed Treecreeper, Jay, Chaffinch and Hawfinch. This is one of the best places for Levaillant's Green Woodpecker as well as other interesting birds such as the North African race of Great Spotted Woodpecker, Moussier's Redstart, Bonelli's Warbler, Golden Oriole and Cirl Bunting. Raptors include Black and Red Kites, Egyptian Vulture, Short-toed Eagle, Sparrowhawk, Long-legged Buzzard, Booted Eagle and Hobby.

Birds which can be found on or near the stony plateaux include Lesser Kestrel, Little Owl, Roller, Thekla Lark, Woodlark, Skylark, Shorelark (endemic subspecies), Tawny Pipit, Black-eared and Black Wheatears, Melodious and Subalpine Warblers, Spotless Starling and Rock Sparrow. One of the commonest birds is the north-west African race of Wheatear.

A tiny relict population of Demoiselle Cranes may still survive in this region but is highly endangered and any birds seen should be left undisturbed and reported to ICBP (see page 19). It is worth going out at night to listen for Scops, Eagle and Tawny Owls and Nightjar.

As early as September, the first passage migrants arrive and later on, from November, all the wintering species will be observed (in particular European ducks).

Other wildlife   European Pond Terrapins live in the lakes, Iberian Wall Lizards, which are very variable in colour, are abundant on the plateaux and mammals such as Jackal, Fox and Weasel are common. Groups of Barbary Apes are regularly seen in the cedar woods near Ifrane-Azrou. In May and June a lot of orchids flower in the region, including Pink Butterfly, Bug, Robust Marsh and Algerian Butterfly Orchids.

The upper valley of the Moulouya wadi

The Moulouya wadi is the second largest in Morocco. Its upper course crosses vast areas of semi-desert covered with alfa bushes, lying between 900 and 1500 m elevation. This unique region's special habitats contain several interesting passerines.

Location   The most interesting parts of this region are within an area bordered by the towns of Boulemane, Imouzzèr-des-Marmoucha, Missour and Midelt, just to the south-east of the eastern Middle Atlas.

Accommodation   The only hotels close to this region are at Midelt (the three star El Ayachi), Ifrane or Azrou (see page 24). There are no camp sites but there is no difficulty in putting up a tent in the countryside. Cafes are

Key

Surfaced roads

Unsurfaced roads/tracks

Streams (permanent)

Contours

Pass

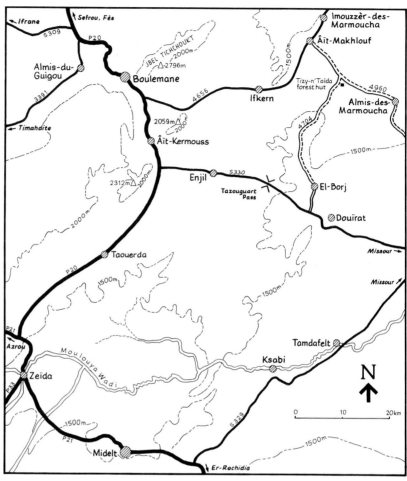

few and it is wise to bring some food either to eat during the day or when camping. The restaurants near the bus station in Midelt serve succulent 'tajines'.

Strategy   There is very little traffic on any of the roads in the region except the P20 and P21, making it difficult to hitch-hike and so it is almost impossible to birdwatch here without a car. Winters are very cold and long on these high plateaux, and summer and autumn are generally very hot and less interesting for the birdwatcher. The best time to birdwatch here is during May and June. In May, it is often possible to birdwatch all day long, but in June the afternoons can sometimes be hot. Stay out until dusk to listen for Eagle Owl and Red-necked Nightjar.

One of the best ways to appreciate the ecological complexity of this area is to drive slowly and observe the distribution and density of birds, especially larks and wheatears. It is worth walking in the alfa steppe to experience this special habitat. If time is available it is worth exploring the mountain tracks to the north-east of Imouzzèr-des-Marmoucha where Booted Eagle, Scops Owl and Subalpine and Orphean Warblers can be seen. The mountains Jbels Bou Iblane and Bou Naceur have been studied by few birdwatchers and may be worth a visit.

Moussier's Redstart

Although it is sometimes possible to find petrol in the villages off the main roads (e.g. at Imouzzèr-des-Marmoucha), it is wise to fill up before leaving the main towns.

Birds

The distribution of birds in this area is governed by altitude, rainfall and vegetation. Larks and wheatears are probably the most fascinating groups of species to observe here.

On the plateaux of the Middle Atlas (along the S309 coming from Ifrane) Skylark, Shorelark, Tawny Pipit, Wheatear (Moroccan race), Black-eared Wheatear and Spotless Starling can be seen.

Several kilometres south of Boulemane the P20 passes through semi-arid and then arid habitats. Follow the P20 or turn east onto the S330. Desert and Temminck's Horned Larks, and Desert and Red-rumped Wheatears can be found here while Shorelarks have disappeared and Skylarks and Black-eared and Black Wheatears are rare. The Wheatear only rarely occurs in this semi-arid habitat and is confined to a few particular places such as around the village of Almis des Marmoucha.

The transitional area between the slopes of the Middle Atlas and the plateaux of the upper Moulouya, where the two avifaunas meet, are particularly interesting. In a small field 5 km north of Taouerda, Crested/Thekla, Calandra and Temminck's Horned Larks and Skylarks have all been seen together in May.

Crested/Thekla Larks are present everywhere, but their identification in the field is very difficult and most birdwatchers only attempt to distinguish them initially.

Besides the already mentioned birds, several other interesting species may be seen in the region. The cliffs and rocks attract raptors such as Black Kite, Egyptian Vulture, Long-legged Buzzard, Booted Eagle, Kestrel and Lanner. Other species found here include Eagle Owl, Crag Martin, Blue Rock Thrush and Rock Sparrow.

Birds of the alfa steppe include Barbary Partridge, Stone-curlew, Black-bellied Sandgrouse, Red-necked Nightjar, Short-toed Lark and Tawny Pipit. Trumpeter Finches are often present in good numbers. This is the best area to look for one of the most poorly known Moroccan birds, Dupont's Lark. During the spring the birds are particularly vocal at dusk and through the night but stop shortly after dawn. Consequently very early morning visits or overnight camping is essential. The plains 3 km to the south of Zeida are one traditional place to look and listen but it may be more widespread as its distribution is poorly known.

The gardens and adjoining areas near the Moulouya wadi (e.g. at Missour or Ksabi) attract various breeding birds among which are Turtle Dove, Bee-eater, Rufous Bush Robin, Nightingale, Olivaceous and Orphean Warblers, Spotted Flycatcher and Great Grey Shrike.

In the mountainous areas to the north of Immouzèr-des-Marmoucha birds such as Hobby, Scops and Little Owls, Nightjar, Redstart and Moussier's Redstart, Melodious, Orphean and Bonelli's Warblers, Woodchat Shrike and Cirl and Rock Buntings can be seen.

During the spring the Moulouya valley acts as a migration corridor for several species: Osprey, Bee-eater, Subalpine and Melodious Warblers.

Other wildlife

Several mammals live in the alfa steppe. Greater Egyptian Jerboa is common and often seen dead on the road. Fox, Jackal and Algerian Hedgehog may also be seen and Leopard has even been reported recently from the holm-oak forest near Imouzzèr-des-Marmoucha. Beware of scorpions which hide under the stones.

Essaouira

The delightful town of Essaouira with its narrow streets, cottage industries (especially cabinet making and inlaid juniper) and fishing harbour, is the best site in Morocco to see the graceful Eleonora's Falcon which is present between May and October.

Location

Essaouira is located on the Atlantic coast 173 km north of Agadir and 176 km west of Marrakech. The city can be easily reached by bus.

Accommodation

There are a number of hotels in the city to cater for the tourist trade. Some are located near the seaside: the three star (A) Tafoukt and the four star (A) Hotels des Iles, while smaller hotels in the old town include the one star (B) Des Remparts and the Smara.

Camping at the municipal camp site is poor and a better choice is the Auberge Camping Tangaro, 5 km before the entrance of the town on the P8 (rooms and restaurant also available).

Some restaurants serve excellent fish and sea-food (e.g. chez Sam, on the harbour), and the open-air ones, near the harbour entrance are also worth trying.

Strategy

The Eleonora's Falcons breed on the islands offshore and the archipelago has recently been set up as a reserve with prohibited access. The best vantage point for viewing the islands is the end of the jetty on the west side of the harbour, and a telescope is essential. A good place to look for the Falcons when they are hunting is the mouth of the Ksob Wadi a few miles to the south which is also a

Key

Surfaced roads	
Unsurfaced roads/tracks	
Open water (permanent)	
Camping	

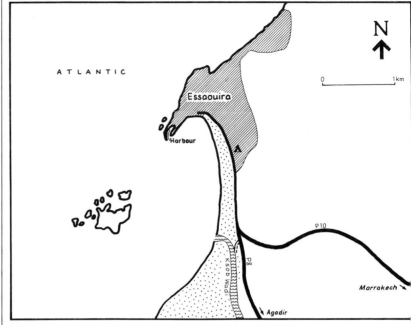

roosting place for waterbirds. The small islets immediately to the west of the harbour, the harbour itself and the bay are worth watching for seabirds.

Birds

One of the best times to visit Essaouira is May and June. The Falcons, which arrive in April, have not yet begun to breed and so do not spend so much time near the islands. In 1986 c90 pairs of Falcons bred. The other breeding birds of the islands are c4000 pairs of Yellow-legged Herring Gulls, some tens of pairs of Cormorants, one pair of Peregrines, Kestrels and Ravens, numerous Rock Doves and several pairs of Pallid Swifts and Sardinian Warblers.

The mouth of the Ksob Wadi is a morning and evening resting place for Yellow-legged Herring Gulls, and Little Egrets, Spoonbills, Avocets and Audouin's Gulls have been noted there. Migrating seabirds which can be seen include Sandwich, Little, Whiskered, Black and White-winged Black Terns.

In the scrub around the mouth of the wadi and in the Juniper woodland along the P8 and the P10 there are Barbary Partridge, Quail, Stone-curlew, Turtle Dove, Common Bulbul, Rufous Bush Robin, Moussier's Redstart, Black-eared Wheatear, Olivaceous and Sardinian Warblers, Spotted Flycatcher, Great Grey and Woodchat Shrikes and Serin.

Pallid Swifts, House Buntings, Spotless Starlings and occasionally Eleonora's Falcons can all be seen while walking round the city.

Other wildlife

In the surrounding countryside Algerian Hedgehog, Brown Hare and Wild Boar are not uncommon. Genets are sometimes seen and some years ago, Caracals were captured.

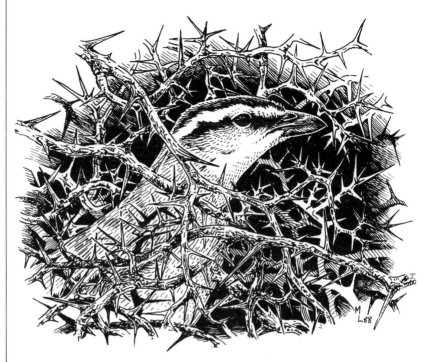

Black-headed
Bush Shrike

Oukaïmeden

This high altitude site in the Toubkal massif of the High Atlas
ranges from 2600 m, where a skiing resort has been built, to 3600 m at
Jbel Angour. About 100 species have been found here including
some of the rarest passerines in the country. At least 50 species breed
(see Barreau et al 1987).

Location

Oukaïmeden is 72 km south of Marrakech but there is no bus
service to it. Traffic is very light except on winter week-ends for
skiing. The only easy way to get to there is by car. Follow the S513
from Marrakech towards the Atlas to the Vallée de l'Ourika. Shortly
after reaching the mountains take the 6035A a good tarmac road on
the right hand side which leads to Oukaïmeden.

Accommodation

Some hotels and restaurants have been built at the resort but are
not always open. Book in advance to stay at the three star (B) Imlil
hotel and the two star (B) chez Juju through a travel agency or the
Syndicat d'Initiative in Marrakech. Accommodation is also available
at the chalet of Club Alpin Français – attractively priced but bedding
is not always supplied, especially in the summer. From spring to
autumn, it is possible to camp near the caravans in the meadow in
front of the resort. It is a good idea to bring food as well as all the
petrol needed for the trip as there are no petrol stations here.

Strategy

The drive from Marrakech takes about 1½ hours so it is possible to
visit the site from there in one day but it is better to spend a couple of
days at this site.

Key

Surfaced roads	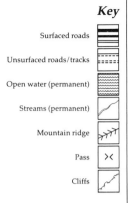
Unsurfaced roads/tracks	
Open water (permanent)	
Streams (permanent)	
Mountain ridge	
Pass	
Cliffs	

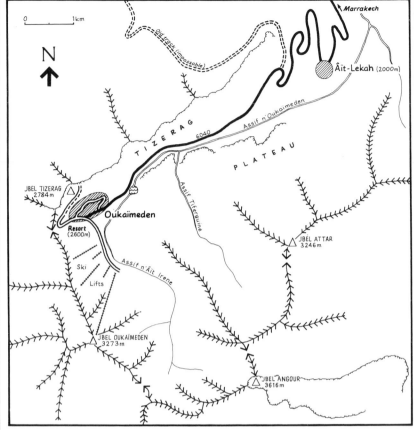

The end of spring, summer and autumn are probably the best seasons to visit the site. Temperatures then are reasonably high – 20–25°C by day and not too cold at night. The sun is almost always out and care should be taken not to get sunburn.

The drive from Marrakech through the plain of Haouz passes through various habitats: arid, with Jujube trees *Ziziphus lotus* up to 900 m; semi-arid with Sandarac trees from 900–1200 m; temperate with Holm Oak from 1200–1900 m; cold semi-arid with Thuriferous Juniper from 1900–2500 m and finally the high mountain layer with low thorny bushes above 2500 m. Each habitat has its own bird community and regular stops should enable a good cross-section of species to be seen.

Birds | On the drive from Marrakech look for: Rufous Bush Robin on the plain; Little Swift, Red-rumped Swallow and the Moroccan race of White Wagtail, mainly in the foothills; Tristram's, Spectacled and Subalpine Warblers in junipers and *Genista*; Black Wheatear and Blue Rock Thrush wherever there are rocks. The very rare White-rumped Swift has been seen near Imlil in the Asni valley, 20 km to the west.

The resort is at the lower limit of the alpine layer. On the plateau to the east there are Alpine Swifts, Tawny Pipits, Black Redstarts, Black Wheatears, Blue Rock Thrushes, Alpine Choughs and Choughs. One of the commonest passerines is the Moroccan race of Wheatear and Shorelark is also abundant, especially on the slopes at the edges of the plateau. The poorly known Crimson-winged Finch can also be seen here and small flocks often occur.

In the village Rock Sparrows are common having colonised the buildings about 20 years ago. A walk towards the summits of the Jbels can be good for seeing Alpine Accentor and Rock Thrush. Lammergeier and Golden Eagle are often seen here. Sunset at the top of Jbel Tizrag, easily accessible by a track, is an unforgettable sight.

Other wildlife

Various reptiles hide amongst the rocks: Colated and Iberian Wall Lizards, and especially the Atlas Gecko, are all common. Barbary Ground-squirrel should not be missed. The rock engravings on the plateau at the east of the resort are worth visiting and look for the Robust Marsh Orchids all along the 'assifs' (streams) in spring.

The lagoons between Sidi-Moussa and Oualidia

This complex system of lagoons and salt pans is an important resting place for numerous migrating birds, and is of special interest for waders. At the present time hunting is forbidden.

Location

The lagoons lie on the Atlantic coast between Sidi Moussa and Oualidia, to the south-west of El-Jadida. The lagoons are best explored by car but they can also be easily reached by bus from El-Jadida and Safi. Buses travel between these two towns on the S121 which runs alongside the lagoons and will stop near the most interesting birdwatching places. It is also possible to reach the site by hitch-hiking.

Accommodation

El-Jadida and Safi are not popular tourist places, and have a fairly poor selection of hotels. Oulidia is a more pleasant place to stay – a popular beach resort with two camping sites and a few hotels/ restaurants; the L'araignée gourmante, the one star Auberge de la Lagune, the two star Hotel Hippocampe. The only hotel/restaurant in Sidi-Moussa is La Brise. It is possible to camp in the open near one of the lagoons.

Oualidia is famous for its oysters which can be bought direct from the farm. There is also a variety of fish and shellfish available.

Strategy

The best times to visit the area are during the peak migration in early spring and autumn. At these times waders are numerous and there are a variety of ducks, raptors and passerines. The lagoons are one of the main wetlands for wintering birds in Morocco and a visit during the winter months is always interesting. Resident passerines such as Crested Lark, Fan-tailed and Sardinian Warblers, Goldfinch and Linnet begin to breed in early March, migrants like Collared Pratincole and Little Tern start later and breeding continues into June. July and August are probably the least interesting months.

Key

Surfaced roads

Unsurfaced roads/tracks

Marsh

Open water (permanent)

Streams (permanent)

Saltpans

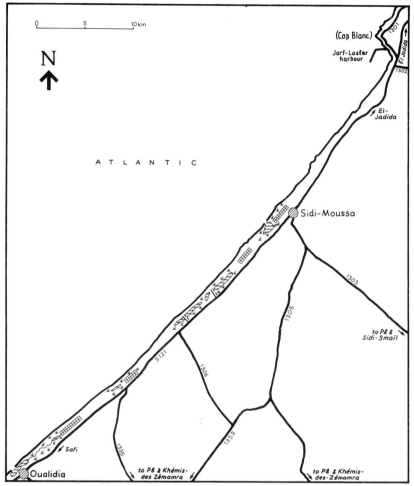

While travelling along the S121 the most interesting places for birds can be clearly seen. Particularly good places are the lagoons near Sidi-Moussa and Oualidia, and the salt pans between these two localities. Various tracks lead to these areas and allow close approach to the birds. The surrounding land can be explored on foot. The mimosa woods on the dunes between the lagoons and the ocean contain large numbers of breeding finches.

The cliffs near the harbour of Jorf-Lasfar (Cap Blanc) are worth visiting as this is a good place for seawatching and Lesser Kestrel, Lanner, Peregrine and Blue Rock Thrush are sometimes seen.

Birds   Cattle and Little Egrets, Grey Herons and White Storks can be seen throughout the year; Little Bitterns and Night, Squacco and Purple Herons are rarer and only seen during migration. Spoonbills and Greater Flamingos are seen almost throughout the year. Some of these birds have been ringed and with a telescope, the number or colour-code of their rings can be seen, showing that the Spoonbills come from the Netherlands and the Flamingos from the Camargue. A wide range of western European ducks, including Marbled Duck, and waders, sometimes including large groups of Black-winged Stilts and Avocets, pass through and winter.

Lesser Crested Tern

The mimosa woods and the adjacent areas attract numerous passerines. In early March the migration of Pallid Swift, Hoopoe, Sedge and Subalpine Warblers and Bluethroat can be seen. Montagu's Harriers pass through in good numbers during the first half of April.

Seawatching can be rewarding with species such as Cory's, Sooty and Manx Shearwaters, Gannet, Cormorant, Caspian and Sandwich Terns, and occasional Lesser Crested and White-winged Black Terns or Audouin's Gulls (113 of the latter flew north in 7½ hours of observation on 1st March 1981). Mediterranean Gulls are sometimes seen at the lagoons in winter, but the only regular Moroccan wintering place for this species is at Sidi Bouzid, a few kilometres south-west of El-Jadida where several hundred birds gather from November to February.

Of the few breeding species, the most interesting are probably Black-winged Stilt, Collared Practincole, Little Tern, Fan-tailed Warbler and Spotless Starling. Montagu's Harrier and African Marsh Owl no longer breed here because of increased disturbance.

This can be a good place to find rare birds. Cape Gannet, Western Reef Heron, Blue-winged Teal, Pectoral Sandpiper, Slender-billed Curlew, Marsh Sandpiper, Laughing Gull, Red-throated Pipit and Scarlet Rosefinch have been seen here.

The mouth of the Oued Massa

The River Massa flows from east to west across the middle of Morocco reaching the Atlantic to the south of Agadir. It is the most northerly Saharan wadi in Morocco. A sand-bank blocks the mouth of the river forming a lake which is connected with the ocean only at the highest tides. Towering sand dunes run along the southern edge

Key

Surfaced roads
Unsurfaced roads/tracks
Marsh
Sand
Sand-dunes
Streams (permanent)
Camping

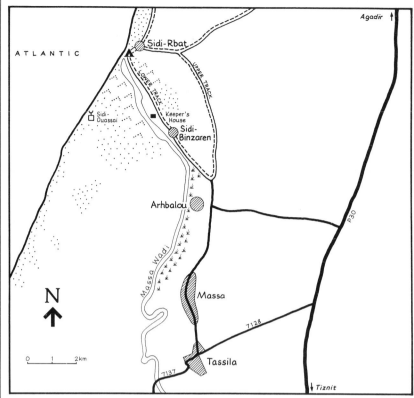

of this lake while the northern shore is fringed with mud banks and flat areas covered with glassworts.

Because of the beautiful landscape and the rich fauna this is one of the most famous birdwatching sites in Morocco. It has been a biological reserve since 1980.

Location

The site is located on the Atlantic coast 40 km south of Agadir. Because it is some distance away from any main roads or towns the easiest way to get there is by car. From Agadir follow the main road (P30) south towards Tiznit and 42 km after Aït-Melloul, take the right hand turning to Tassila. Once in the village, turn right and drive north. This small road passes through the village of Massa and shortly after the village of Arhbalou (on the left) it splits into two. The mouth of the Massa can be reached along either of these two tracks but generally only one is navigable depending on local conditions – beware of the frequent accumulations of sand on the road. On the way back it is possible to take the new road that leads from Arhbalou directly to the P30 but this small road is hard to find from the P30 end.

Accommodation

The only accommodation available near the mouth is a camp site. Here you can either use your own tent or can rent one of the few bungalows that are available. You should not camp anywhere other than in the camp site. Sometimes the owner of the camp site is willing to prepare meals but it is wise to bring your own supply of food from Agadir, Tassila or Massa.

Bald Ibis

Do not bathe in the wadi as it is forbidden and there is a risk of disease. Be very careful in the ocean as there are strong currents close to shore.

Strategy

The site can be visited for a day from Agadir but its ornithological richness often deserves greater attention and a stay of several days is worthwhile. The best times to visit the site are between September and November and between February and April when many migrants are present. The winter period from October to March is also very productive. A visit during March will produce a lot of migrating and wintering species and some will also be breeding.

It is possible to birdwatch throughout the day, except during the hotter summer months. In the early morning it is worth sitting concealed near the mouth of the river to wait for the Black-bellied Sandgrouse which come in to drink each day, approximately two hours after sunrise. Then walk along the track on the north side of the river but don't go right down to the shore as this might flush the feeding waders and waterfowl as well as annoy the warden. From November to early March Cranes fly in and spend the day in the reeds in the middle of the river across from the warden's house. They generally arrive between 10.00 and 11.00 and leave before sunset. Up to 200 birds have been counted in the winter.

If time is available follow the track back to the point where the river turns south away from the track and look carefully in the reeds for species such as Little Bittern. It is also worth walking across the desert areas to the north-east to look for Stone-curlews, Cream-coloured Coursers and larks.

Birds

During the winter the last five km of the river hold an important population of Coots (c8,000) and numerous ducks (3–5,000). Most of the commoner European species are present as are some more unusual ones such as Ruddy Shelduck, Marbled Duck, Red-crested Pochard and Ferruginous Duck. The sand bank at the mouth of the river acts as a roosting place for gulls and terns (sometimes more than 2,000 birds). The commonest are Lesser Black-backed and Yellow-legged Herring Gulls, but several other species are regularly seen including Audouin's and Little Gulls and Caspian and Sandwich Terns. The large number of birds at the site attract several raptors and Marsh Harrier, Tawny, Booted and Bonelli's Eagles and Peregrine and Barbary Falcons are all seen regularly.

The spring migration of some species starts as early as December. At that time the first Swallows heading north sometimes meet the last Swallows heading south! At Christmas the first Great Spotted Cuckoos, Pallid Swifts, Hoopoes, Red-rumped Swallows, House Martins and Reed Warblers appear. Migration continues until April. From February/March likely species include Little Bittern, Night, Squacco and Purple Herons, Glossy Ibis, Spoonbill, Spotted and Baillon's Crakes, Gull-billed Tern, Bee-eater, Black-eared Wheatear and various warblers, including Olivaceous, Spectacled and Sub-alpine.

Breeding begins in March. Among the more interesting breeding species are Barbary Partridge, Stone-curlew, Cream-coloured Courser, Little Owl, Moussier's Redstart, Fan-tailed Warbler, Black-headed Bush Shrike, Great Grey Shrike, Spotless Starling and House Bunting. Brown-throated Sand Martin breeds throughout the year.

Several species that do not actually breed at the site regularly visit it to roost or feed, all year. These include Little Egret, Bald Ibis, Greater Flamingo, Osprey and Black-bellied Sandgrouse.

Because of the heat the summer is the least productive period. Post-breeding movements start in August but it is not until November that large numbers of birds are once again present at the site.

Many rare birds have been found at this site including some seldom seen elsewhere in the Western Palearctic. Western Reef Heron, Great White Egret, Lesser Flamingo, Fulvous Whistling Duck, Snow Goose, Spur-winged Goose, American Wigeon, Green-winged and Blue-winged Teals, Ring-necked Duck, Pallid Harrier, Allen's Gallinule, Long-billed Dowitcher and White-tailed Plover are just some of them. Keep a careful look out for such rarities.

Other wildlife

Several mammals are common here and these include Algerian Hedgehog, Brown Hare, Barbary Ground-squirrel, Jackal, Red Fox, Weasel, Egyptian Mongoose and African Wild Cat. Amphibians and reptiles are abundant and include Green Toad, Edible Frog, Stripe-necked Terrapin, Helmeted, Dwarf and Moorish Geckos, Bibron's Agama, Ocellated, Orange-tailed and Senegal Skinks, and Rough and Leopard Lizards. The Egyptian Cobra is known from the vicinity.

The plain of the Sous

No one should visit southern Morocco without visiting the area around the River Sous. This plain, between the High and the Anti-Atlas, with its fruit orchards and vegetable cultivations is one of the richest areas of Morocco, but little by little the expansion of this agriculture is destroying a very unique habitat, the argana forest. The Sous is nevertheless still one of the most famous ornithological regions of the country.

Location

The region lies inland of Agadir and is bisected by the P32 which runs east from Agadir to Ouarzazate. It can also be reached from Marrakech to the north-east along the S501 which crosses the High Atlas and climbs up to 2092 m at the Tizi-n-Test pass which is often blocked by snow in January/February. This route passes through wonderful landscapes and provides a charming view over the plain. The size of the region makes a car essential.

Key

Surfaced roads

Seasonal water

Pass

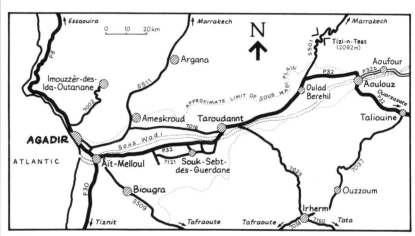

Accommodation

The closest tourist area is Agadir where hotels are numerous but often full and booking in advance through a travel agent is advisable. Taroudannt, the historic capital of the Sous, lies at the centre of the region and has a number of hotels. The cheapest hotels (low or medium category) are in the medina; the four star Hotel Salam and La Gazelle d'Or are outside the walls of the city (this last hotel is one of the most famous and expensive in Morocco). Coming from Ouarzazate, the four star Hotel Ibn Toumert in Taliouine is a good place to stay. A quiet place to camp can easily be found in the argana forest.

Strategy

The region contains a wide variety of habitats and several interesting or uncommon species. It is best to spend a few days here, even though it can be covered in one or two days.

Like most sites, the Sous is best visited in spring, but shouldn't be ignored at other times of year. It is possible to birdwatch throughout the day except during the hot summer months. During April and May stay in the argana forest until dusk to listen for Stone-curlew, Little Owl or Red-necked Nightjar.

Black-shouldered
Kite

The argana forest is the habitat that generally attracts birdwatch-ers, and it is certainly one of the most interesting. Other areas such as the olive groves, with their huge trees, the area around the Sous wadi and the south-western slopes of the High Atlas are all worth exploring. The Anti-Atlas, to the south, especially in its central and northern parts, is poorly known zoologically and the authors wel-come details of any interesting observations from here. The roads and tracks in this area are in bad condition.

Birds

Except in some remote areas, the argana forest has been degraded due to man or livestock. Tree-climbing goats are a frequent sight beside the road in this area. Nevertheless many interesting species such as Stone-curlew, Red-necked Nightjar, Moussier's Redstart, Black-headed Bush Shrike and Magpie (Moroccan race) can be seen close to the main roads. This is one of the best areas for Tawny Eagle and two nests were found here in 1981.

The orchards and hedges contain lots of passerines, especially finches and they also form one of the favourite habitats of the Black-shouldered Kite.

Old olive groves, such as the ones that can be found some kilometres south of the P32 (along any of the numerous roads or tracks that go southwards) form a very pleasant habitat. Lots of birds can be seen here, especially during migration. Common breeding birds include Common Bulbul, Rufous Bush Robin, Olivaceous Warbler, Spotted Flycatcher and various finches. Most sightings of Dark Chanting Goshawk are from this region and although it has not been proven to breed in Morocco as yet, it may do so in this habitat. Perhaps the best place to see this species (and Black-shouldered Kite) is along the P32 near Taroudannt. In the town itself Pallid Swift and Spotless Starling can be seen.

The cliffs at the foothills of the Atlas are good for breeding raptors: Egyptian and Griffon Vultures (only one or two pairs of the latter), Long-legged Buzzard, Golden, Booted and Bonelli's Eagles, Kestrel, Lanner, Peregrine and Barbary Falcon can all be seen here.

One of the most famous breeding colonies of Bald Ibis was located near Aoulouz, above the bridge over the Sous wadi. During recent years only a few pairs have bred irregularly and two old nest sites can still be seen from the bridge. A dam is now being built here and this will destroy the site. Some individuals are regularly seen feeding in the wadi, west of the bridge.

The mouth of the Sous wadi

The River Sous flows into the Atlantic just south of Agadir. The mouth of the river is very wide with mud and sandbanks. This is an important resting place for numerous waders, gulls and terns and is well worth visiting.

Location

Agadir is one of the main tourist centres in Morocco and can be easily reached by plane or road. Buses run to here from most other towns in Morocco. The site can be reached by taking the main road south-east from town. Just before Inezgane, near the airport, several roads on the right-hand side lead south to a track that runs along the northern bank of the wadi towards the mouth.

Accommodation

In Agadir there is a wide selection of accommodation, with hotels up to five star, many restaurants and a camping site. It is inadvisable to camp near the river mouth. It is also possible to visit this site while based at the camp site near the mouth of Oued Massa (see page 35).

Strategy

The migration periods, from February to April and September to November, are the best times to visit, but the winter can also be

Key

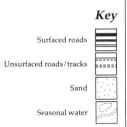

Surfaced roads

Unsurfaced roads/tracks

Sand

Seasonal water

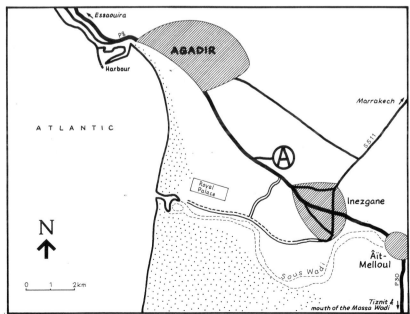

interesting, especially at the end of the year when the first migrants appear. Summer is probably the least interesting time. Visit the site in the early morning, when there are fewer people and less disturbance. Remember to lock cars when leaving them.

Three or four hours are generally enough time to spend here. Other places nearby worth visiting include Agadir harbour, where Little, Glaucous and Great Black-backed Gulls and Kittiwake have been seen and Cape Rhir, 40 km north of the city on the P8, where commoner seabirds as well as rarities, which have included Black-browed Albatross and Bulwer's Petrel, can be seen on seawatches.

Birds

Most of the small European waders can be seen here, and other species include Cormorant, Little Egret, White Stork, Spoonbill, Greater Flamingo, Black-winged Stilt and Avocet. Bald Ibis and Ruddy Shelduck are frequently seen in winter.

The mouth is very good for gulls and terns, which use the sand banks as roosting places. Black-headed, Lesser Black-backed and Yellow-legged Herring Gulls and Sandwich Tern are the commonest, but it is not unusual to find one or more of the following species: Mediterranean, Little, Slender-billed, Audouin's and Great Black-backed Gulls and Gull-billed, Caspian, Royal, Lesser Crested, Common, Arctic, Little, Whiskered, Black and White-winged Black Terns, especially in winter and spring.

The nearby bushes and wooded areas are excellent places to look for migrant passerines. Some interesting resident species are: Brown-throated Sand Martin, Moussier's Redstart, Black-headed Bush Shrike and Great Grey Shrike. House Bunting is common wherever there are houses, especially in Agadir.

Some uncommon or vagrant species which have been seen here are Lesser Flamingo, Spur-winged Goose, Great Knot and Plain Swift.

Ouarzazate

To the east of Ouarzazate lies the El Mansour Eddahbi dam which collects the waters from various rivers, in particular the Dadès, to form a large reservoir of variable extent. Below the dam runs the Oued Drâa which waters a splendid valley, before vanishing under the Drâa hamada near Mhamid, and re-appearing to flow into the Atlantic.

The site is interesting not only because the dam forms the only large and permanent body of water in the sub-desert area south of the central High Atlas, but also because several desert birds can be observed nearby. The area around the lake, which appears dry and stony, with only a few bushes, shelters a surprisingly rich bird community.

Location

Ouarzazate stands on the crossroads where the road along the southern side of the High Atlas, from Agadir to Figuig (P32) crosses the P31 which runs from Marrakech to the Drâa valley. It can easily

Key

Surfaced roads

Unsurfaced roads/tracks

Open water (permanent)

Seasonal water

Dam/barrage

Camping

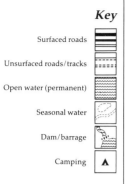

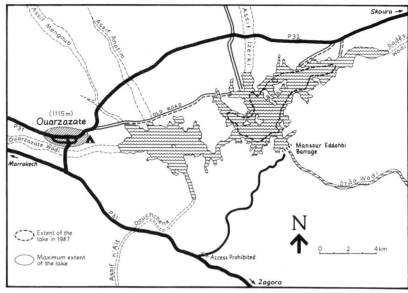

be reached by bus, especially from Marrakech. The reservoir can be easily reached from the P32 along several roads and tracks which lead to the northern shore. Access to the southern side, from the P31, is much more difficult and not recommended. Access to the dam itself is forbidden.

Accommodation

Ouarzazate has a wide variety of hotels. Of the cheaper hotels the two star (B) La Gazelle, at the west entrance of the city, is recommended while the more expensive four star (A) Azghor, at the east of the town, has a swimming pool and is smarter. Restaurants are fairly numerous. A good camp site is at the east end of town, near the municipal swimming-pool which is often empty.

Thick-billed Lark

Strategy

Because of its geographical position, Ouarzazate is a strategic overnight stop when travelling through southern Morocco. March and April are the best months for migrants and May is best for breeding birds. Avoid travelling in this region between June and September, because of the heat.

Try to arrive here in the afternoon as a visit to the site in the evening can be interesting, when migrants stop here before crossing the Atlas the next morning. The following morning drive east for some kilometres on the old road which approaches the reservoir at various points depending on the level of water. The best places for birds will have to be searched for as they vary. Be wary of the mud which can sometimes be invisible. At the eastern end of the reservoir, where the Dadès river flows in, a lot of birds sometimes gather. This area can be reached from the P32 and overhanging cliffs allow easy observation.

Don't forget to look for passerines in the desert areas around the reservoir.

If time is available it is worth making a two day trip down the Drâa valley, to Tamegroute (184 km) and back. The side road (6956) east to Nekob, which starts 98 km south of Ouarzazate on the P31, is worth exploring for sandgrouse and other desert species. A good day trip is to visit Marrakech (204 km) over the Tichka pass (2260 m), on a splendid road through the Atlas which is sometimes obstructed by snow in winter.

Birds

The lake is a roosting and feeding place for wintering and migrating ducks and waders. In the early spring, there are often Spoonbills and Greater Flamingos at the eastern tip while White Storks, Black-winged Stilts and Avocets can be seen anywhere.

In March and April there are many migrating species, especially raptors such as Black Kite, Short-toed Eagle, Montagu's Harrier and Booted Eagle as well as Bee-eater, Short-toed and Lesser Short-toed Larks, hirundines, Black-eared Wheatear, warblers and Woodchat Shrike.

Few water birds breed although this is the only breeding site for Grey Heron in Morocco. Ruddy Shelducks are fairly common with up to 400 in December. Among the commonest resident passerines are Desert Lark, White-crowned Black Wheatear and Trumpeter Finch. Spotted and Black-bellied Sandgrouse, Bar-tailed Desert, Hoopoe and Thick-billed Larks and Mourning Wheatear can sometimes be seen here.

Osprey, Marsh Harrier, Long-legged Buzzard, Lanner and Peregrine/Barbary Falcon are seen fairly frequently. Rarities have included White Pelican and Grey Phalarope.

Rock Martins, which occur in southern Morocco, probably reach their northernmost limit just to the south of the Tinififft pass c50 km south of Ouarzazate on the P31. A few birds have been reliably identified here by visiting birdwatchers.

Other wildlife

You will notice numerous rodent burrows, mainly belonging to Shaw's Jird.

Valleys and gorges of the Todra and Dadès wadis

These two rivers rise in the central part of the High Atlas. They pass through impressive gorges and irrigate lush, green valleys. The Dadès gorge has many local fortified villages (kasbahs), and the Todra valley is lined with one of the nicest palm-groves in the country. This beautiful landscape is worth visiting in itself and is a good example of the habitats to be found in the valleys of the southern foothills of the High Atlas. The more adventurous bird-watcher might consider driving from one valley to the other via Tamtattouchte. The desert immediately to the south of the P32, between the two valleys, is one of the most accessible in Morocco and is the best place to see a range of desert birds.

Location

Access to the valleys starts from the towns of Boumalne du Dadès and Tinerhir, on the main P32 that runs along the south side of the High Atlas. The two towns can be reached by bus (2–3 per day) but a car is really necessary to explore the area. The gorges can be reached by taxi but their prices can be exorbitant for tourists. From Boumalne the S6901 runs up the Dadès gorge and from Tinerhir the S6902 leads to the Todra gorge (tarmac up to the gorge). The desert to the south is best explored along the track to Tagdilt which runs south-east, leaving the P32 a few kilometres east of Boumalne, opposite a garage.

Key

Surfaced roads	
Unsurfaced roads/tracks	
Palms	
Seasonal water	
Pass	

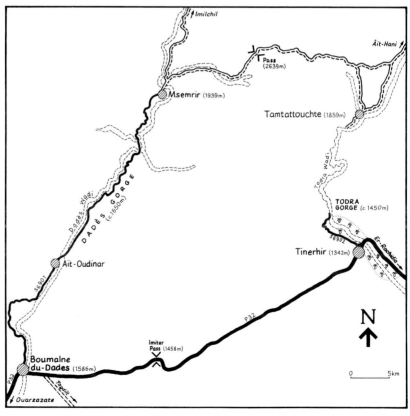

Accommodation

Boumalne has only one hotel, the four star (B) Madayaq which is rather expensive for the quality offered. In the Dadès valley itself, the only place to stay is the simple but clean Auberge des gorges du Dadès at Aït-Oudinar, 22 km from Boumalne. Tinerhir has more hotels such as the Todra, the De l'Oasis or the Saghro and a camp site set in the palm-grove. There are several restaurants. The Todra valley has some nice camp sites including the Atlas and the Source des poissons sacrés as well as some small hotels/restaurants. Inside the gorge itself there are two small hotels, the Yasmina and the des roches. There is one hotel/restaurant/camp site at Tamtattouchte. When sleeping in the valleys away from Boumalne or Tinerhir, remember that the nights are cool and a sleeping bag will be needed.

Strategy

The best time to visit the lower valleys is from March to May and the mountains are best from May to July. It is worth spending at least two days here. One day should be spent in the palm-groves and in the Todra gorge and the other exploring the Dadès valley.

If you intend to drive the circuit between the two valleys through the Atlas, start at Tinerhir, going through Tamtattouchte and Msemrir to Boumalne. The most difficult part of the route is in the Todra valley. Only a quarter of the 140 km route is tarmac and while it can be driven in one day, it would be better to take two. A Renault 4 is generally sufficient.

Birds

In the palm-groves and fields of the lower valleys White Stork, Hoopoe, Common Bulbul, Blackbird, Cetti's Warbler, Blue Tit and Raven are all common.

At the gorges Golden and Bonelli's Eagles and Lammergeiers are sometimes seen. In the Todra gorge there are colonies of House Martins and Crag Martins, and some birdwatchers have claimed Rock Martins as well though this has yet to be proved.

Going further north into the gorges the rocky plateaux, screes, and scrub vegetation contain such species as Barbary Partridge, Black and Moussier's Redstarts, Black Wheatear, Blue Rock Thrush, Spectacled Warbler, Chough, and Rock and House Buntings, or perhaps the last of the wintering Ring Ouzels and even Desert Larks (up to c2200 m, despite its name). One of the most interesting species here is probably the Crimson-winged Finch and Tristram's Warbler is sometimes seen.

Above 2600 m Shorelark and the North African race of Wheatear can be found among the high altitude xerophytic vegetation.

Travelling south down the Dadès valley from Msemrir the fields and trees along the wadi contain Quail, Golden Oriole, Cetti's and Reed Warblers, Serin and Goldfinch as well as Rock Sparrow and Trumpeter Finch.

In the desert south of the P32, to the east of Boumalne du Dadès, a number of species which can be hard to find elsewhere in Morocco can be seen. These are Hoopoe, Thick-billed and Temminck's Horned Larks and Red-rumped Wheatear. Houbara Bustard used to be quite common in this area but sadly the species has undergone a dramatic decline due to winter hunting by Arab falconers. If seen these birds should not be disturbed. Other species here include Long-legged Buzzard, Lanner, Cream-coloured Courser and Desert, Mourning and White-crowned Black Wheatears. At night the small and pale North African race of Eagle Owl can be heard and recently Dupont's Lark has been discovered near Boumalne.

The Tafilalt

The Tafilalt is the region closest to the Sahara, centred on the towns of Erfoud and Rissani. Once famous for its trade in gold, ivory and ebony, it nowadays offers the birdwatcher an opportunity to see a wide range of Saharan desert species.

Location

The region lies very close to the Algerian border, in the south-east of Morocco, where the main roads from the north and west come to an end.

There are two routes leading to Erfoud: the main P21 that comes from the north, via Er Rachidia and follows the Ziz wadi, and the 3451 that starts at Tinejdad on the P32, 55km east of Tinehir. These two roads pass through attractive landscapes and, if using a car, it is worth arriving by one route and leaving by the other.

Erfoud can also be reached by bus from Er Rachidia and a Land-Rover and driver can be hired for a one-day trip out into the desert. Land-Rovers can be booked from hotel reception desks.

The region can also be reached from the P31 (Ouarzazate-Zagora road) along the 3454, a track which is only tarmac in parts. Although it is an interesting route, the track is in fairly poor condition, and is only recommended to those who have previous experience of similar

Key

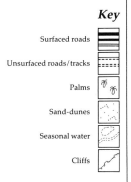

Surfaced roads

Unsurfaced roads/tracks

Palms

Sand-dunes

Seasonal water

Cliffs

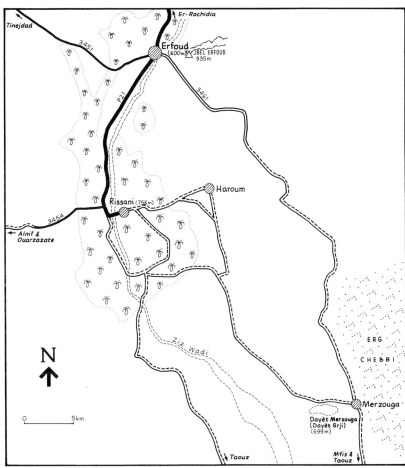

Desert Sparrow

journeys. A four-wheel drive vehicle is best and two days should be allowed. Remember to take spare wheels and plenty of petrol, food and water.

Accommodation

There are not many hotels in Erfoud, and their prices are rather high considering their standard and the frequent water shortages. In recent years, the Hotel des Palmiers, in the main street, was the best value for money. The four star Sijilmassa is often full in March and April, and it is necessary to book a room in advance.

There is a very modest camp site at Erfoud, and another between Erfoud and Er Rachidia, at Source bleue de Meski. In Merzouga, there is simple accommodation at the small cafe/restaurant.

Strategy

Two to three days are necessary to explore the Tafilalt thoroughly. April and May are probably the best months to visit this region. November to February can also be interesting, but the summer visitors are absent. Avoid the period from June to October when it is very hot and uncomfortable for birdwatching.

In spring, especially in May, it is best to start birdwatching at dawn as by mid-morning it can be quite hot, the birds are less mobile and the heat haze becomes a problem. On hot days it is a good idea to rest in the middle of the day and to start birdwatching again in the late afternoon.

The three main habitats in the region are the palm-groves, the stone deserts and the sand-dunes. Each of them contain their own distinct avifauna. Palm-groves are found all along the Ziz wadi; the only major sand-dune system in Morocco, the Erg Chebbi, is situated to the east of Merzouga and everywhere else is stone desert.

Numerous tracks cross the desert making it easy to get lost. Before setting out, check petrol levels and the condition of the spare wheel. When there is a sand storm do not venture out.

One of the best tracks to explore is the 3461 which leads from Erfoud to Merzouga, and is tarmac for some distance. Don't drive too far south as the area close to the Algerian border is rather sensitive. It is best to stay within the limits of the map (see page 47). Even those with their own transport should consider renting a Land-Rover and driver for their first trip into the desert.

After a rainy winter, the Dayèt (lake) of Merzouga, which forms in the open desert is worth a visit as it attracts Greater Flamingos, ducks and waders.

Birds

The palm-groves and adjacent areas along the Ziz wadi attract birds such as Barbary Partridge, Moorhen, Turtle Dove, Scops Owl, Tawny Owl (recently discovered here), Hoopoe, the Moroccan race of White Wagtail, Common Bulbul, Rufous Bush Robin and Cetti's and Olivaceous Warblers during the breeding season. In migration periods, numerous passerines stop to feed.

The dunes of the Erg Chebbi are relatively poor for birds but the landscape is unique in Morocco and worth experiencing. Only six species breed: Bar-tailed Desert, Hoopoe, Short-toed and Crested Larks, Desert Warbler and Desert Sparrow. The tamarisks that fringe the dunes at Merzouga are a very good place to observe wintering Tristram's Warblers, from mid-November to late April (mainly from December to February).

Although some birds are very conspicuous, many of the species which inhabit the vast tracts of stone desert can be difficult to find. Regular breeding birds include Stone-curlew, Crowned and Black-bellied Sandgrouse, Bar-tailed Desert, Desert and Hoopoe Larks, Desert, Mourning and White-crowned Black Wheatears, Scrub Warbler, Desert Sparrow and Trumpeter Finch. The Houbara Bustard is now very rare because of hunting. There have been reports of Arabian Bustards in the desert around Merzouga several times in recent years. Its exact status is unclear and details of any sightings should be sent to the author. Cream-coloured Courser, Spotted and Pin-tailed Sandgrouse, Egyptian Nightjar, Thick-billed, Short-toed and Temminck's Horned Larks, and Spectacled Warbler only breed in certain years, depending on climatic conditions.

Long-legged Buzzard, Kestrel and Lanner breed in the region and just to the north, Egyptian Vulture, Bonelli's Eagle and Peregrine also breed. Short-toed and Tawny Eagles are regularly observed in spring, but breeding has never been proved. Honey Buzzard, Black Kite, Montagu's Harrier, Booted Eagle, Osprey and Hobby are regular passage migrants, and Marsh Harrier and Sparrowhawk regularly winter.

Species which can be found in gardens, palm-groves, cliffs or stone desert include Barn, Eagle and Little Owls, Blue-cheeked Bee-eater and Bee-eater, Crag Martin, Fulvous Babbler, Great Grey Shrike, Brown-necked Raven and Raven.

If there is water in the Dayèt of Merzouga, try to arrive there at sunrise. White Stork, Greater Flamingo, Ruddy Shelduck, Wigeon, Gadwall, Teal, Mallard, Pintail, Avocet, Ringed Plover, Little Stint, Ruff, Bar-tailed and Black-tailed Godwits, Spotted Redshank, Redshank, Greenshank and Common Sandpiper can all be seen and the presence of so many waterbirds in the open desert is an unforgett-able sight. Black-winged Stilt, Kentish Plover and Gull-billed Tern have been noted breeding here during particularly wet years.

Other species   Several reptiles will probably be seen and the most conspicuous are the Agamas and the Spiny-tailed Lizard.

Bald Ibis. Once much commoner, only ten colonies are currently occupied. In 1981, 354 birds were counted but there were only 69 breeding pairs. One of the most famous colonies is at Aoulouz (page 39), which is nowadays only occupied irregularly and will soon be destroyed by the construction of a dam. It occurs regularly at the mouth of the Sous wadi (page 41) in winter and at the mouth of the Oued Massa (page 35) throughout the year.

Marbled Duck. An uncommon bird, except in a few places such as Lac de Sidi Bourhaba (page 20) where it breeds and wintering numbers can reach several hundred. The mouth of the Oued Massa (page 35) is another good place to find it although it doesn't breed. Birds wander and from time to time can even be seen on temporary lakes in desert areas e.g. the Dayèt of Merzouga in the Tafilalt (page 47).

Black-shouldered Kite. An uncommon local resident with a stable population of 100–500 pairs. It is found in three distinct areas: the plains and hills of the NW (including Zaërs, page 22), Marrakech region and Sous (page 39). Inhabits open ground, arable and grassland with trees and hedges; also in palm-groves near Marrakech.

Dark Chanting Goshawk. A very scarce resident breeder, with an estimated population of a few dozen pairs. Restricted to the plain of the Sous (page 39) and perhaps the western fringe of the High Atlas, in argana forest and olive-groves. Its biology in Morocco is almost unknown.

Tawny Eagle. A very rare resident breeder, with an estimated population of a few dozen pairs. Found in the past, over a large part of Morocco, it is now scarce and probably restricted to the plain of the Sous (page 39). From time to time it is seen in other parts of the country, especially the Tafilalt (page 47). In winter it is often seen at the mouth of the Oued Massa (page 35).

Eleonora's Falcon. A very rare migrant breeder which arrives at its colonies from late April and leaves in the second half of October. There are only two colonies: the coastal cliffs of Salé, near Rabat (21–25 pairs in 1981) and the islands off Essaouira (c200 pairs in 1958, 45–50 pairs in 1980, 90 pairs in 1986) (page 29).

Peregrine/Barbary Falcon. A common resident and rare winter visitor, throughout the whole of Morocco. Although currently split into two species, the races which occur in Morocco can be very difficult to separate in the field. Consequently their distribution is poorly understood. At least five 'types' of birds occur, including *peregrinus* (winter), *brookei*, *pelegrinoides*, *minor* and other undescribed forms.

Double-spurred Francolin. A rare resident in the Zaërs (page 22), the Central Plateau and the plain of the Sous (page 39). In the Zaërs the population is increasing due to the creation of 'hunting reserves'. It is now regularly seen or heard near Sidi-Bettache, Ben Slimane and

Sidi-Yahya-des-Zaërs, in suitable habitat – cork oak woods with dense undergrowth, especially near small wadis.

Helmeted Guineafowl. Until 1920 the species was common in the Zaërs, the Central Plateau and the western foothills of the Middle Atlas. The population gradually decreased and the species has disappeared from Morocco. The last records of wild birds were in 1973 and recent sightings are almost certainly of birds which have escaped from farms.

Andalusian Hemipode. A very rare resident, whose biology is almost unknown in Morocco. Nowadays it appears to be restricted to two regions, the eastern Mediterranean coast near the mouth of Moulouya wadi and the Atlantic coast between Casablanca and Safi.

Crested Coot. A local resident, common on certain lakes such as those of the Middle Atlas (page 24) or Lac de Sidi Bourhaba (page 20).

Demoiselle Crane. A very rare migrant breeder; restricted to the Middle Atlas, where only a small endangered population, now estimated at 10–20 birds, survives.

Houbara Bustard. Previously, a common resident on the eastern High Plateaux and in the southern deserts. Nowadays, because of over-hunting, especially by Middle Eastern falconers, the species has become very rare. Most recent records come from the steppes of the East and the Tafilalt (page 47).

Arabian Bustard. Previously common in uncultivated steppes of most of Morocco. Now very rare. Recent records from desert areas south of the Atlas from the Oued Massa (page 35) to the Tafilalt (page 47).

Great Bustard. A small relict population still survives in the north, in fields near Larache. It has been seen once at Merdja Zerga (page 17).

Slender-billed Curlew. Commonly reported as wintering species until the 1960's. Since then it has declined markedly, with only 17 records in the 1970's. The few records since 1980 come from the estuaries and marshes of NW Morocco including Merdja Zerga (page 17), Casablanca, the lagoons between Sidi Moussa and Oualidia (page 33) and the mouth of the Oued Massa (page 35).

Audouin's Gull. It breeds only on the Mediterranean coast, where the largest colony is located on the Chafarines islands, off the mouth of Moulouya wadi (2220 nests in 1981). It winters mainly along the Mediterranean coast with smaller numbers along the Atlantic coast, although several hundred birds were seen around 28°N in the 1985/86 winter. It is seen throughout the year at the mouth of the Oued Massa (page 35), and mainly during migration periods at Merdja Zerga (page 17), the lagoons between Sidi Moussa and Oualidia (page 33), and the mouth of the Sous wadi (page 41).

Lichtenstein's Sandgrouse. A resident, strictly associated with the occurrence of *Acacia seyal* in the stone desert south of the Jbel Bani, in the far south of Morocco.

Crowned Sandgrouse. A resident which inhabits all the desert areas south of a line from Goulimime in the south-west, through Zagora and Merzouga to Figuig. Outside the breeding season it can be observed on the eastern High Plateaux as far north as Aïn-Benimathar (34°N).

Spotted Sandgrouse. A resident, whose breeding distribution in Morocco is very similar to that of the previous species. Outside the breeding season, it may wander to the eastern High Plateaux, in the region of Ouarzazate (page 42) and in the plain of the Sous (page 39).

Black-bellied Sandgrouse. A resident which occurs in the eastern High Plateaux (up to the Mediterranean coast), the Rharb, the Haouz, the plain of the Sous (page 39) and the southern foothills of the High Atlas, in particular around Ouarzazate (page 42). It does not occur south of Erfoud, Zagora and Goulimime.

Pin-tailed Sandgrouse. A resident in the steppes of the eastern High Plateaux and the near-desert south of the High and Anti-Atlas. Like the Crowned and Spotted Sandgrouse it wanders in relation to climatic conditions.

African Marsh Owl. A rare resident, restricted to certain places within the Tanger-Casablanca-Meknès triangle. This owl has suffered from the destruction and drainage of its marshy habitat. A few pairs still survive at Lac de Sidi Bourhaba (page 20) and a larger population occurs at Merdja Zerga (page 17).

Egyptian Nightjar. A migrant breeder. Nowadays, mainly seen in the Tafilalt (page 47), where it is present from mid-March to mid-August, but only seems to breed during wet years. It is generally found on fairly sandy soils, but also on stone desert and even in palm-groves. It bred south-west of Marrakech in the 60's.

White-rumped Swift. A very rare migrant breeder, probably restricted to a few valleys in the central High Atlas. It has been recorded in the Asni and Ourika valleys, south of Marrakech and in the mountains to the north-west of Ouarzazate. Almost nothing is known about its biology in Morocco.

Blue-cheeked Bee-eater. A migrant breeder, present only in the Figuig region in the far south-east, in the Tafilalt (page 47) and in the lower Drâa valley. It arrives at the end of March and is seen until the end of September. It breeds in the banks of the wadis and the slopes of the irrigation channels, sometimes alongside the Bee-eater. It is frequently seen on wires beside roads.

Dupont's Lark. The least known lark in Morocco. It inhabits the steppes of the eastern High Plateaux, and extends up the upper valley of the Moulouya wadi (page 26), where most of the recent sightings come from. Quite recently, it has been seen near Taliouine, between Ouarzazate and Taroudant, and near Boumalne (page 45).

Thick-billed Lark. A resident, which wanders outside the breeding season. This large lark occurs through the semi-desert and desert areas of the eastern High Plateaux and south of the High Atlas, on stone desert and hamadas from Ouarzazate to the Tafilalt (page 42–47). In autumn and winter, birds can gather in flocks up to several dozen.

Rock Martin. A bird of uncertain status, this Saharan species seems to be restricted to the borders of the north-western Sahara. The only proven breeding records come from the Figuig region, south-east Morocco (old records), and from the western Sahara. Most sightings in the foothills of High Atlas (in particular those of Todra and Dadès valleys) very probably refer to Crag Martins. The species has been seen on the P31 to the south of Ouarzazate (page 42).

Scrub Warbler. A resident, patchily distributed, mainly in the steppes of semi-desert areas south of the High Atlas, sometimes in the foothills. Often seen in the south-east between Tinerhir and Erfoud (page 45) and in the region of Goulimime in the south-west.

Tristram's Warbler. An altitudinal migrant which only breeds in the maquis of the High Atlas between 1200 m and 2400 m. South of the Atlas, it is only a winter visitor and is common from December to February in the tamarisk near Merzouga (page 47).

Desert Warbler. It is restricted to sandy soils of desert areas and generally considered as resident, but mainly seen from January to June in the Tafilalt (page 47), where it is fairly common.

Fulvous Babbler. A fairly common resident in all the semi-desert and desert areas south of the High Atlas, from the Figuig in the south-east to the western Sahara, through the Tafilalt (page 47), the Drâa valley and the plain of the Sous (page 39). It inhabits open land with scattered bushes and shrubs and open palm-groves. The species is gregarious and is generally met with in groups of up to 10–15 birds.

Black-headed Bush Shrike. A fairly common local resident, known from Tanger east along the Mediterranean coast and up into the Rif, the Zaërs (page 22), the Central Plateau, the area around Essaouira (page 29) and the plain of the Sous (page 39) and the nearby coast. It lives in scrub, and in spring, it is most easily located by its voice.

Desert Sparrow. An uncommon resident. It reaches one of its north-west limits in the Tafilalt (page 47), where it occurs around the Erg Chebbi. In winter, it sometimes mixes with flocks of House Sparrows and can be seen near the cafe north of Merzouga.

Crimson-winged Finch. A rare resident, confined to high altitudes in the Middle Atlas, such as Jbel Bou Iblane, and the High Atlas. One of the best places to observe the species is around Oukaimeden (page 31), where it can be seen from 2300 m to 3000 m in the breeding season, and down to 1400 m in winter.

This list includes the 414 species that have been noted at least once in Morocco north of parallel 28°N (i.e. excluding Western Sahara) during the 20th century. It does not take into account species whose sightings records have not been documented enough to be accepted. A code gives the present status of each species north of parallel 28°N.

The following code has been chosen:

Key to Checklist

rb   resident breeder
ob   occasional breeder
fb   former breeder, disappeared
mb   migrant breeder, present only in breeding period
pm   passage migrant
wv   regular winter visitor
as   accidental species
1   very common
2   common
3   fairly common
4   uncommon
5   rare or very localised

as ☐	Red-throated Diver (Gavia stellata)
as ☐	Black-throated Diver (Gavia arctica)
as ☐	Great Northern Diver (Gavia immer)
rb2wv2 ☐	Little Grebe (Tachybaptus ruficollis)
rb3wv3 ☐	Great Crested Grebe (Podiceps cristatus)
rb4wv3 ☐	Black-necked Grebe (Podiceps nigricollis)
as ☐	Black-browed Albatross (Diomedea melanophris)
as ☐	Fulmar (Fulmarus glacialis)
as ☐	Bulwer's Petrel (Bulweria bulwerii)
mb5pm3 ☐	Cory's Shearwater (Calonectris diomedea)
pm4 ☐	Great Shearwater (Puffinus gravis)
pm4 ☐	Sooty Shearwater (Puffinus griseus)
pm3wv3 ☐	Manx Shearwater (Puffinus puffinus)
as ☐	Little Shearwater (Puffinus assimilis)
pm5 ☐	Wilson's Petrel (Oceanites oceanicus)
as ☐	White-faced Petrel (Pelagodroma marina)
pm3wv3 ☐	Storm Petrel (Hydrobates pelagicus)
pm4 ☐	Leach's Petrel (Oceanodroma leucorhoa)
as ☐	Madeiran Petrel (Oceanodroma castro)
as ☐	Cape Gannet (Sula capensis)
as ☐	Masked Booby (Sula dactylatra)
pm1wv1 ☐	Gannet (Sula bassana)
rb3wv2 ☐	Cormorant (Phalacrocorax carbo)
rb5wv4 ☐	Shag (Phalacrocorax aristotelis)
as ☐	Long-tailed Cormorant (Phalacrocorax africanus)
as ☐	Darter (Anhinga melanogaster)
as ☐	White Pelican (Pelecanus onocrotalus)
rb5pm4 ☐	Bittern (Botaurus stellaris)
mb3pm3 ☐	Little Bittern (Ixobrychus minutus)
mb3pm3 ☐	Night Heron (Nycticorax nycticorax)
mb4pm3 ☐	Squacco Heron (Ardeola ralloides)
rb1 ☐	Cattle Egret (Bubulcus ibis)

as ☐	Western Reef Heron (Egretta gularis)
rb1wv1 ☐	Little Egret (Egretta garzetta)
as ☐	Great White Egret (Egretta alba)
pm1wv1ob ☐	Grey Heron (Ardea cinerea)
pm3mb3 ☐	Purple Heron (Ardea purpurea)
as ☐	Yellow-billed Stork (Mycteria ibis)
pm4 ☐	Black Stork (Ciconia nigra)
mb1pm1 ☐	White Stork (Ciconia ciconia)
pm4wv4 ☐	Glossy Ibis (Plegadis falcinellus)
rb5mb5 ☐	Bald Ibis (Geronticus eremita)
pm3wv3 ☐	Spoonbill (Platalea leucorodia)
pm1wv1ob ☐	Greater Flamingo (Phoenicopterus ruber)
as ☐	Lesser Flamingo (Phoenicopterus minor)
as ☐	Fulvous Whistling Duck (Dendrocygna bicolor)
as ☐	Mute Swan (Cygnus olor)
as ☐	Whooper Swan (Cygnus cygnus)
as ☐	Bean Goose (Anser fabalis)
as ☐	White-fronted Goose (Anser albifrons)
wv4 ☐	Greylag Goose (Anser anser)
as ☐	Snow Goose (Anser caerulescens)
as ☐	Barnacle Goose (Branta leucopsis)
rb3 ☐	Ruddy Shelduck (Tadorna ferruginea)
wv3 ☐	Shelduck (Tadorna tadorna)
as ☐	Spur-winged Goose (Plectropterus gambensis)
as ☐	Mandarin (Aix galericulata)
wv1 ☐	Wigeon (Anas penelope)
as ☐	American Wigeon (Anas americana)
wv2rb5 ☐	Gadwall (Anas strepera)
wv1 ☐	Teal (Anas crecca)
rb1wv1 ☐	Mallard (Anas platyrhynchos)
wv2ob ☐	Pintail (Anas acuta)
pm2 ☐	Garganey (Anas querquedula)
as ☐	Blue-winged Teal (Anas discors)
as ☐	Cape Shoveler (Anas smithii)
wv1ob ☐	Shoveler (Anas clypeata)
rb3wv3 ☐	Marbled Duck (Marmaronetta angustirostris)
wv4rb5 ☐	Red-crested Pochard (Netta rufina)
wv2ob ☐	Pochard (Aythya ferina)
as ☐	Ring-necked Duck (Aythya collaris)
rb5wv4 ☐	Ferruginous Duck (Aythya nyroca)
wv3 ☐	Tufted Duck (Aythya fuligula)
as ☐	Scaup (Aythya marila)
wv2 ☐	Common Scoter (Melanitta nigra)
as ☐	Goldeneye (Bucephala clangula)
wv5 ☐	Red-breasted Merganser (Mergus serrator)
fb ☐	White-headed Duck (Oxyura leucocephala)
pm2 ☐	Honey Buzzard (Pernis apivorus)
rb4 ☐	Black-shouldered Kite (Elanus caeruleus)
mb1pm1 ☐	Black Kite (Milvus migrans)
rb5wv4 ☐	Red Kite (Milvus milvus)
rb5 ☐	Lammergeier (Gypaetus barbatus)
mb3pm2 ☐	Egyptian Vulture (Neophron percnopterus)
pm5wv5ob ☐	Griffon Vulture (Gyps fulvus)
fb ☐	Lappet-faced Vulture (Torgos tracheliotus)
as ☐	Black Vulture (Aegypius monachus)

mb2pm2 □	Short-toed Eagle (Circaetus gallicus)
rb2wv2 □	Marsh Harrier (Circus aeruginosus)
wv4 □	Hen Harrier (Circus cyaneus)
as □	Pallid Harrier (Circus macrourus)
mb3pm2 □	Montagu's Harrier (Circus pygargus)
rb5 □	Dark Chanting Goshawk (Melierax metabates)
rb4wv4 □	Goshawk (Accipiter gentilis)
rb2wv2 □	Sparrowhawk (Accipiter nisus)
wv3pm3 □	Buzzard (Buteo buteo)
rb5 □	Long-legged Buzzard (Buteo rufinus)
as □	Spotted Eagle (Aquila clanga)
rb5 □	Tawny Eagle (Aquila rapax)
asfb □	Imperial Eagle (Aquila heliaca)
rb3 □	Golden Eagle (Aquila chrysaetos)
mb2pm2 □	Booted Eagle (Hieraaetus pennatus)
rb2 □	Bonelli's Eagle (Hieraaetus fasciatus)
rb5pm3wv3 □	Osprey (Pandion haliaetus)
mb2pm2 □	Lesser Kestrel (Falco naumanni)
rb1wv1 □	Kestrel (Falco tinnunculus)
as □	Red-footed Falcon (Falco vespertinus)
wv5 □	Merlin (Falco columbarius)
mb3pm3 □	Hobby (Falco subbuteo)
mb5 □	Eleonora's Falcon (Falco eleonorae)
rb2 □	Lanner (Falco biarmicus)
as □	Saker (Falco cherrug)
rb2wv3 □	Peregrine Falcon (Falco peregrinus)
rb3 □	Barbary Falcon (Falco pelegrinoides)
rb1 □	Barbary Partridge (Alectoris barbara)
rb4 □	Double-spurred Francolin (Francolinus bicalcaratus)
mb2pm2 □	Quail (Coturnix coturnix)
rb4 □	Pheasant (Phasianus colchicus)
fb □	Helmeted Guineafowl (Numida meleagris)
rb5 □	Andalusian Hemipode (Turnix sylvatica)
rb4wv3 □	Water Rail (Rallus aquaticus)
pm4 □	Spotted Crake (Porzana porzana)
pm4 □	Little Crake (Porzana parva)
mb5pm4 □	Baillon's Crake (Porzana pusilla)
wv4 □	Corncake (Crex crex)
rb1 □	Moorhen (Gallinula chloropus)
as □	Allen's Gallinule (Porphyrula alleni)
rb3 □	Purple Gallinule (Porphyrio porphyrio)
rb1wv1 □	Coot (Fulica atra)
rb3 □	Crested Coot (Fulica cristata)
wv4 □	Crane (Grus grus)
mb5 □	Demoiselle Crane (Anthropoides virgo)
rb4wv4 □	Little Bustard (Tetrax tetrax)
rb5 □	Houbara (Chlamydotis undulata)
fb □	Arabian Bustard (Ardeotis arabs)
rb5 □	Great Bustard (Otis tarda)
wv2pm2 □	Oystercatcher (Haematopus ostralegus)
mb2pm2wv4 □	Black-winged Stilt (Himantopus himantopus)
wv2pm2ob □	Avocet (Recurvirostra avosetta)
rb2wv2 □	Stone-curlew (Burhinus oedicnemus)
rb3 □	Cream-coloured Courser (Cursorius cursor)
mb3pm3 □	Collared Pratincole (Glareola pratincola)

rb3pm4 ☐	Little Ringed Plover (Charadrius dubius)
wv1pm1 ☐	Ringed Plover (Charadrius hiaticula)
rb1wv1 ☐	Kentish Plover (Charadrius alexandrinus)
wv5 ☐	Dotterel (Charadrius morinellus)
wv2 ☐	Golden Plover (Pluvialis apricaria)
wv1pm1 ☐	Grey Plover (Pluvialis squatarola)
as ☐	Sociable Plover (Chettusia gregaria)
as ☐	White-tailed Plover (Chettusia leucura)
rb5wv2 ☐	Lapwing (Vanellus vanellus)
as ☐	Great Knot (Calidris tenuirostris)
pm3wv3 ☐	Knot (Calidris canutus)
wv1 ☐	Sanderling (Calidris alba)
pm1wv1 ☐	Little Stint (Calidris minuta)
pm4 ☐	Temminck's Stint (Calidris temminckii)
as ☐	Pectoral Sandpiper (Calidris melanotos)
pm4wv4 ☐	Curlew Sandpiper (Calidris ferruginea)
as ☐	Purple Sandpiper (Calidris maritima)
wv1pm1 ☐	Dunlin (Calidris alpina)
as ☐	Broad-billed Sandpiper (Limicola falcinellus)
pm2wv4 ☐	Ruff (Philomachus pugnax)
wv4 ☐	Jack Snipe (Lymnocryptes minimus)
wv1 ☐	Snipe (Gallinago gallinago)
wv5 ☐	Great Snipe (Gallinago media)
as ☐	Long-billed Dowitcher (Limnodromus griseus)
wv3 ☐	Woodcock (Scolopax rusticola)
wv1pm1 ☐	Black-tailed Godwit (Limosa limosa)
pm2wv3 ☐	Bar-tailed Godwit (Limosa lapponica)
pm2wv2 ☐	Whimbrel (Numenius phaeopus)
wv5 ☐	Slender-billed Curlew (Numenius tenuirostris)
pm2wv3 ☐	Curlew (Numenius arquata)
pm3wv3 ☐	Spotted Redshank (Tringa erythropus)
wv2pm2 ☐	Redshank (Tringa totanus)
pm5 ☐	Marsh Sandpiper (Tringa stagnatilis)
pm3wv3 ☐	Greenshank (Tringa nebularia)
as ☐	Lesser Yellowlegs (Tringa flaviceps)
wv2pm2 ☐	Green Sandpiper (Tringa ochropus)
pm3wv3 ☐	Wood Sandpiper (Tringa glareola)
pm2wv4 ☐	Common Sandpiper (Actitis hypoleucos)
pm2wv2 ☐	Turnstone (Arenaria interpres)
as ☐	Wilson's Phalarope (Phalaropus tricolor)
wv5 ☐	Red-necked Phalarope (Phalaropus lobatus)
wv5 ☐	Grey Phalarope (Phalaropus fulicarius)
pm5 ☐	Pomarine Skua (Stercorarius pomarinus)
pm4 ☐	Arctic Skua (Stercorarius parasiticus)
as ☐	Long-tailed Skua (Stercorarius longicaudus)
pm4 ☐	Great Skua (Stercorarius skua)
wv4 ☐	Mediterranean Gull (Larus melanocephalus)
as ☐	Laughing Gull (Larus atricilla)
pm4wv4 ☐	Little Gull (Larus minutus)
pm5 ☐	Sabine's Gull (Larus sabini)
wv1 ☐	Black-headed Gull (Larus ridibundus)
as ☐	Grey-headed Gull (Larus cirrocephalus)
rb5 ☐	Slender-billed Gull (Larus genei)
rb4wv4 ☐	Audouin's Gull (Larus audouinii)
as ☐	Ring-billed Gull (Larus delawarensis)

wv5 ☐	Common Gull (Larus canus)
wv1pm1 ☐	Lesser Black-backed Gull (Larus fuscus)
wv5 ☐	Herring Gull (Larus argentatus)
rb1 ☐	Yellow-legged Herring Gull (Larus cachinnans)
as ☐	Iceland Gull (Larus glaucoides)
as ☐	Glaucous Gull (Larus hyperboreus)
wv5 ☐	Great Black-backed Gull (Larus marinus)
wv5 ☐	Kittiwake (Rissa tridactyla)
pm3ob ☐	Gull-billed Tern (Gelochelidon nilotica)
wv4 ☐	Caspian Tern (Sterna caspia)
pm4 ☐	Royal Tern (Sterna maxima)
pm4 ☐	Lesser Crested Tern (Sterna bengalensis)
pm2wv3 ☐	Sandwich Tern (Sterna sandvicensis)
pm5 ☐	Roseate Tern (Sterna dougallii)
pm3wv5ob ☐	Common Tern (Sterna hirundo)
pm5 ☐	Arctic Tern (Sterna paradisaea)
mb3pm3 ☐	Little Tern (Sterna albifrons)
pm3wv5fb ☐	Whiskered Tern (Chlidonias hybridus)
pm2 ☐	Black Tern (Chlidonias niger)
pm5 ☐	White-winged Black Tern (Chlidonias leucopterus)
as ☐	Guillemot (Uria aalge)
wv4 ☐	Razorbill (Alca torda)
wv5 ☐	Puffin (Fratercula arctica)
rb5 ☐	Lichtenstein's Sandgrouse (Pterocles lichtensteinii)
rb4 ☐	Crowned Sandgrouse (Pterocles coronatus)
rb3 ☐	Spotted Sandgrouse (Pterocles senegallus)
rb2 ☐	Black-bellied Sandgrouse (Pterocles orientalis)
rb3 ☐	Pin-tailed Sandgrouse (Pterocles alchata)
rb1 ☐	Rock Dove (Columba livia)
rb4 ☐	Stock Dove (Columba oenas)
rb3wv3 ☐	Woodpigeon (Columba palumbus)
as ☐	Collared Dove (Streptopelia decaocto)
mb1pm1 ☐	Turtle Dove (Streptopelia turtur)
rb5 ☐	Laughing Dove (Streptopelia senegalensis)
as ☐	Namaqua Dove (Oena capensis)
pm3 ☐	Great Spotted Cuckoo (Clamator glandarius)
pm1mb2 ☐	Cuckoo (Cuculus canorus)
as ☐	Yellow-billed Cuckoo (Coccyzus americanus)
rb2 ☐	Barn Owl (Tyto alba)
pm2mb3 ☐	Scops Owl (Otus scops)
rb4 ☐	Eagle Owl (Bubo bubo)
rb2 ☐	Little Owl (Athene noctua)
rb3 ☐	Tawny Owl (Strix aluco)
rb4wv4 ☐	Long-eared Owl (Asio otus)
pm4wv4 ☐	Short-eared Owl (Asio flammeus)
rb5 ☐	African Marsh Owl (Asio capensis)
pm3mb4 ☐	Nightjar (Caprimulgus europaeus)
mb3wv5 ☐	Red-necked Nightjar (Caprimulgus ruficollis)
mb5 ☐	Egyptian Nightjar (Caprimulgus aegyptius)
as ☐	Plain Swift (Apus unicolor)
pm1mb3 ☐	Swift (Apus apus)
mb2pm2 ☐	Pallid Swift (Apus pallidus)
mb3pm3 ☐	Alpine Swift (Apus melba)
mb5 ☐	White-rumped Swift (Apus caffer)
mb3rb3 ☐	Little Swift (Apus affinis)

rb3wv3 ☐	Kingfisher (Alcedo atthis)
mb4 ☐	Blue-cheeked Bee-eater (Merops superciliosus)
mb2pm2 ☐	Bee-eater (Merops apiaster)
mb3pm3 ☐	Roller (Coracias garrulus)
mb3pm2 ☐	Hoopoe (Upupa epops)
pm3wv5 ☐	Wryneck (Jynx torquilla)
rb3 ☐	Levaillant's Green Woodpecker (Picus vaillantii)
rb3 ☐	Great Spotted Woodpecker (Dendrocopos major)
rb2 ☐	Bar-tailed Desert Lark (Ammomanes cincturus)
rb2 ☐	Desert Lark (Ammomanes deserti)
rb3 ☐	Hoopoe Lark (Alaemon alaudipes)
rb4 ☐	Dupont's Lark (Chersophilus duponti)
rb3 ☐	Thick-billed Lark (Rhamphocoris clotbey)
rb2 ☐	Calandra Lark (Melanocorypha calandra)
mb2 ☐	Short-toed Lark (Calandrella brachydactyla)
rb3 ☐	Lesser Short-toed Lark (Calandrella rufescens)
rb1 ☐	Crested Lark (Galerida cristata)
rb1 ☐	Thekla Lark (Galerida theklae)
rb3 ☐	Woodlark (Lullula arborea)
rb4wv4 ☐	Skylark (Alauda arvensis)
rb3 ☐	Shore Lark (Eremophila alpestris)
rb3 ☐	Temminck's Horned Lark (Eremophila bilopha)
rb2 ☐	Brown-throated Sand Martin (Riparia paludicola)
pm2ob ☐	Sand Martin (Riparia riparia)
rb5 ☐	Rock Martin (Ptyonoprogne fuligula)
rb3wv3 ☐	Crag Martin (Ptyonoprogne rupestris)
mb2pm1 ☐	Swallow (Hirundo rustica)
mb3pm3 ☐	Red-rumped Swallow (Hirundo daurica)
mb2pm1 ☐	House Martin (Delichon urbica)
as ☐	Richard's Pipit (Anthus novaeseelandiae)
mb3pm3 ☐	Tawny Pipit (Anthus campestris)
pm3 ☐	Tree Pipit (Anthus trivialis)
wv1 ☐	Meadow Pipit (Anthus pratensis)
wv5 ☐	Red-throated Pipit (Anthus cervinus)
wv4 ☐	Water Pipit (Anthus spinoletta)
wv4 ☐	Rock Pipit (Anthus petrosa)
mb2pm2wv4 ☐	Yellow Wagtail (Motacilla flava)
rb3wv3 ☐	Grey Wagtail (Motacilla cinerea)
rb3wv2 ☐	White Wagtail (Motacilla alba)
rb1 ☐	Common Bulbul (Pycnonotus barbatus)
rb4 ☐	Dipper (Cinclus cinclus)
rb4 ☐	Wren (Troglodytes troglodytes)
as ☐	Dunnock (Prunella modularis)
rb4wv4 ☐	Alpine Accentor (Prunella collaris)
mb2 ☐	Rufous Bush Robin (Cercotrichas galactotes)
rb3wv2 ☐	Robin (Erithacus rubecula)
mb2pm2 ☐	Nightingale (Luscinia megarhynchos)
pm4wv4 ☐	Bluethroat (Luscinia svecica)
wv2rb4 ☐	Black Redstart (Phoenicurus ochruros)
mb4pm3 ☐	Redstart (Phoenicurus phoenicurus)
rb2 ☐	Moussier's Redstart (Phoenicurus moussieri)
pm3 ☐	Whinchat (Saxicola rubetra)
rb2wv2 ☐	Stonechat (Saxicola torquata)
as ☐	Isabelline Wheatear (Oenanthe isabellina)
pm2mb3rb5 ☐	Wheatear (Oenanthe oenanthe)

mb3pm3 ☐	Black-eared Wheatear (Oenanthe hispanica)
mb2rb4 ☐	Desert Wheatear (Oenanthe deserti)
rb3 ☐	Red-rumped Wheatear (Oenanthe moesta)
rb4 ☐	Mourning Wheatear (Oenanthe lugens)
rb2 ☐	White-crowned Black Wheatear (Oenanthe leucopyga)
rb2 ☐	Black Wheatear (Oenanthe leucura)
mb3pm3 ☐	Rock Thrush (Monticola saxatilis)
rb2 ☐	Blue Rock Thrush (Monticola solitarius)
wv3 ☐	Ring Ouzel (Turdus torquatus)
rb1 ☐	Blackbird (Turdus merula)
as ☐	Fieldfare (Turdus pilaris)
wv3pm3 ☐	Song Thrush (Turdus philomelos)
wv4 ☐	Redwing (Turdus iliacus)
rb3wv3 ☐	Mistle Thrush (Turdus viscivorus)
rb2 ☐	Cetti's Warbler (Cettia cetti)
rb2 ☐	Fan-tailed Warbler (Cisticola juncidis)
rb3 ☐	Scrub Warbler (Scotocerca inquieta)
pm4wv5 ☐	Grasshopper Warbler (Locustella naevia)
as ☐	River Warbler (Locustella fluviatilis)
pm4mb4 ☐	Savi's Warbler (Locustella luscinioides)
rb4 ☐	Moustached Warbler (Acrocephalus melanopogon)
pm5 ☐	Aquatic Warbler (Acrocephalus paludicola)
pm3 ☐	Sedge Warbler (Acrocephalus schoenobaenus)
as ☐	Marsh Warbler (Acrocephalus palustris)
mb3pm3 ☐	Reed Warbler (Acrocephalus scirpaceus)
mb3pm3 ☐	Great Reed Warbler (Acrocephalus arundinaceus)
mb2 ☐	Olivaceous Warbler (Hippolais pallida)
as ☐	Icterine Warbler (Hippolais icterina)
mb3pm3 ☐	Melodious Warbler (Hippolais polyglotta)
as ☐	Marmora's Warbler (Sylvia sarda)
rb3wv3 ☐	Dartford Warbler (Sylvia undata)
mb3 ☐	Tristram's Warbler (Sylvia deserticola)
mb3 ☐	Spectacled Warbler (Sylvia conspicillata)
mb3pm2 ☐	Subalpine Warbler (Sylvia cantillans)
rb1 ☐	Sardinian Warbler (Sylvia melanocephala)
rb4 ☐	Desert Warbler (Sylvia nana)
mb4pm4 ☐	Orphean Warbler (Sylvia hortensis)
as ☐	Lesser Whitethroat (Sylvia curruca)
mb4pm4 ☐	Whitethroat (Sylvia communis)
pm3 ☐	Garden Warbler (Sylvia borin)
pm2wv1rb4 ☐	Blackcap (Sylvia atricapilla)
as ☐	Dusky Warbler (Phylloscopus fuscatus)
mb3pm3 ☐	Bonelli's Warbler (Phylloscopus bonelli)
pm4 ☐	Wood Warbler (Phylloscopus sibilatrix)
wv1pm2rb5 ☐	Chiffchaff (Phylloscopus collybita)
pm3 ☐	Willow Warbler (Phylloscopus trochilus)
as ☐	Goldcrest (Regulus regulus)
rb3 ☐	Firecrest (Regulus ignicapillus)
mb3pm3 ☐	Spotted Flycatcher (Muscicapa striata)
as ☐	Red-breasted Flycatcher (Ficedula parva)
as ☐	Semi-collared Flycatcher (Ficedula semitorquata)
as ☐	Collared Flycatcher (Ficedula albicollis)
mb3pm3 ☐	Pied Flycatcher (Ficedula hypoleuca)
as ☐	Bearded Tit (Panurus biarmicus)
rb3 ☐	Fulvous Babbler (Turdoides fulvus)

as ☐	Long-tailed Tit (Aegithalos caudatus)
as ☐	Crested Tit (Parus cristatus)
rb2 ☐	Coal Tit (Parus ater)
rb2 ☐	Blue Tit (Parus caeruleus)
rb2 ☐	Great Tit (Parus major)
rb3 ☐	Nuthatch (Sitta europaea)
as ☐	Wallcreeper (Tichodroma muraria)
rb2 ☐	Short-toed Treecreeper (Certhia brachydactyla)
as ☐	Penduline Tit (Remiz pendulinus)
mb3pm3 ☐	Golden Oriole (Oriolus oriolus)
rb4 ☐	Black-headed Bush Shrike (Tchagra senegala)
as ☐	Red-backed Shrike (Lanius collurio)
rb1 ☐	Great Grey Shrike (Lanius excubitor)
mb2pm2 ☐	Woodchat Shrike (Lanius senator)
rb2 ☐	Jay (Garrulus glandarius)
rb3 ☐	Magpie (Pica pica)
rb3 ☐	Alpine Chough (Pyrrhocorax graculus)
rb3 ☐	Chough (Pyrrhocorax pyrrhocorax)
rb3 ☐	Jackdaw (Corvus monedula)
as ☐	Carrion Crow (Corvus corone)
rb3 ☐	Brown-necked Raven (Corvus ruficollis)
rb2 ☐	Raven (Corvus corax)
wv2 ☐	Starling (Sturnus vulgaris)
rb3 ☐	Spotless Starling (Sturnus unicolor)
rb1 ☐	House Sparrow (Passer domesticus)
rb1 ☐	Spanish Sparrow (Passer hispaniolensis)
rb5 ☐	Desert Sparrow (Passer simplex)
asob ☐	Tree Sparrow (Passer montanus)
rb3 ☐	Rock Sparrow (Petronia petronia)
as ☐	Senegal Firefinch (Lagonosticta senegala)
as ☐	Red-eyed Vireo (Vireo olivaceus)
rb1wv1 ☐	Chaffinch (Fringilla coelebs)
wv5 ☐	Brambling (Fringilla montifringilla)
rb1wv2 ☐	Serin (Serinus serinus)
rb1wv2 ☐	Greenfinch (Carduelis chloris)
rb1wv2 ☐	Goldfinch (Carduelis carduelis)
wv4 ☐	Siskin (Carduelis spinus)
rb2wv3 ☐	Linnet (Acanthis cannabina)
as ☐	Redpoll (Acanthis flammea)
rb4wv4 ☐	Crossbill (Loxia curvirostra)
rb4 ☐	Crimson-winged Finch (Rhodopechys sanguinea)
rb2 ☐	Trumpeter Finch (Bucanetes githagineus)
as ☐	Scarlet Rosefinch (Carpodacus erythrinus)
as ☐	Bullfinch (Pyrrhula pyrrhula)
rb3wv3 ☐	Hawfinch (Coccothraustes coccothraustes)
as ☐	Snow Bunting (Plectophenax nivalis)
rb3 ☐	Cirl Bunting (Emberiza cirlus)
rb3 ☐	Rock Bunting (Emberiza cia)
rb2 ☐	House Bunting (Emberiza striolata)
pm4 ☐	Ortolan Bunting (Emberiza hortulana)
rb4wv4 ☐	Reed Bunting (Emberiza schoeniclus)
rb1 ☐	Corn Bunting (Emberiza calandra)

AMPHIBIANS AND REPTILES

adapted from Bons 1967

Urodeles
- ☐ Sharp-ribbed Salamander   (Pleurodeles waltli)
- ☐ Salamander   (Salamandra algira)

Anoures
- ☐ Painted Frog   (Discoglossus pictus)
- ☐ Midwife Toad   (Alytes obstetricans)
- ☐ Varaldi's Spade-foot Toad   (Pelobates varaldii)
- ☐ Common Toad   (Bufo bufo)
- ☐ Green Toad   (Bufo viridis)
- ☐ Brongersma's Toad   (Bufo brongersmai)
- ☐ Moroccan Toad   (Bufo mauritanicus)
- ☐ Stripeless Tree Frog   (Hyla meridionalis)
- ☐ Edible Frog   (Rana ridibunda)

Chelonians
- ☐ Stripe-necked Terrapin   (Clemmys caspica)
- ☐ European Pond Terrapin   (Emys orbicularis)
- ☐ Spur-thighed Tortoise   (Testudo graeca)
- ☐ Loggerhead Turtle   (Caretta caretta)
- ☐ Leathery Turtle   (Dermochelys coriacea)

Saurians
- ☐ Helmeted Gecko   (Gekonia chazaliae)
- ☐ Turkish Gecko   (Hemidactylus turcicus)
- ☐ Fan-footed Gecko   (Ptyodactylus hasselquisti)
- ☐ Atlas Gecko   (Quedenfeldtia trachyblepharus)
- ☐ Lizard-toed Gecko   (Saurodactylus fasciatus)
- ☐ Dwarf Gecko   (Saurodactylus mauritanicus)
- ☐ Petrie's Gecko   (Stenodactylus petriei)
- ☐ Elegant Gecko   (Stenodactylus stenodactylus)
- ☐ White-spotted Gecko   (Tarentola annularis)
- ☐ Desert Gecko   (Tarentola ephippiata)
- ☐ Moorish Gecko   (Tarentola mauritanica)
- ☐ Tripoli Pigmy Gecko   (Tropiocolotes tripolitanus)
- ☐ Bibron's Agama   (Agama bibroni)
- ☐ Changeable Agama   (Agama mutabilis)
- ☐ Spiny-tailed Lizard   (Uromastix acanthinurus)
- ☐ Mediterranean Chameleon   (Chameleo chameleon)
- ☐ Three-toed Skink   (Chalcides chalcides)
- ☐ Atlas Skink   (Chalcides atlantis)
- ☐ Golden-striped Skink   (Chalcides mionecton)
- ☐ Ocellated Skink   (Chalcides ocellatus)
- ☐   (Chalcides polylepis)
- ☐   (Chalcides viridanus)
- ☐ Orange-tailed Skink   (Eumeces schneideri)
- ☐ Sandfish   (Scincus scincus)
- ☐ Senegal Skink   (Sphenops sphenopsiformis)
- ☐ Barbary Skink   (Sphenops boulengeri)

- ☐ Rough Lizard   (Acanthodactylus boskianus)
- ☐ Spiny-footed Lizard   (Acanthodactylus erythrurus)
- ☐ Savigny's Lizard   (Acanthodactylus savignyi)
- ☐ Leopard Lizard   (Acanthodactylus pardalis)
- ☐   (Acanthodactylus scutellatus)
- ☐ Fringe-toed Lizard   (Acanthodactylus inornatus)
- ☐   (Acanthodactylus longipes)
- ☐ Small-spotted Lizard   (Eremias guttulata)
- ☐ Pasteur's Spotted Lizard   (Eremias pasteuri)
- ☐   (Eremias olivieri)
- ☐ Red-spotted Lizard   (Eremias rubropunctata)
- ☐ Iberian Wall Lizard   (Podarcis hispanica)
- ☐ Colated (Ocellated) Lizard   (Lacerta lepida)
- ☐ Moroccan Rock Lizard   (Lacerta perspicillata)
- ☐ Atlas Lizard   (Lacerta andreanski)
- ☐ Ophiops   (Ophiosops occidentalis)
- ☐ Large Psammodromus   (Psammodromus algirus)
- ☐ Algerian Psammodromus   (Psammodromus blanci)
- ☐ Small-toed Psammodromus   (Psammodromus microdactylus)
- ☐ Moroccan Glass Lizard   (Ophisaurus koellikeri)
- ☐ Desert Monitor   (Varanus griseus)
- ☐ Amphisbaenian   (Blanus cinereus)
- ☐ Trogonophis   (Trogonophis wiegmanni)

Ophidians

- ☐ Beaked-thread Snake   (Leptotyphlops macrorhynchus)
- ☐ Javelin Sand Boa   (Eryx jaculus)
- ☐ African Common Snake   (Boaedon fuliginosum)
- ☐ Algerian Whip Snake   (Coluber algirus)
- ☐ Horseshoe Snake   (Coluber hippocrepis)
- ☐ Southern Smooth Snake   (Coronella girondica)
- ☐ Diademed Sand Snake   (Lytorhynchus diadema)
- ☐ False Smooth Snake   (Macroprotodon cucullatus)
- ☐ Moila Snake   (Malpolon moilensis)
- ☐ Montpellier Snake   (Malpolon monspessulanus)
- ☐ Viperine Snake   (Natrix maura)
- ☐ Grass Snake   (Natrix natrix)
- ☐ Schokari Sand Snake   (Psammophis schokari)
- ☐ Long-marked Snake   (Sphalerosophis dolichospilus)
- ☐ Diadem Whip Snake   (Sphalerosophis diadema)
- ☐ Egg-eating Snake   (Dasypeltis scabra)
- ☐ Egyptian Cobra   (Naja haje)
- ☐ Puff Adder   (Bitis arietans)
- ☐ Greater-horned Sand Viper   (Cerastes cerastes)
- ☐ Lesser-horned Sand Viper   (Cerastes vipera)
- ☐ Carpet Viper   (Echis carinatus)
- ☐ Lataste's Viper   (Vipera latastei)
- ☐   (Vipera lebetina)

MAMMALS

adapted from Aulagnier and Thévenot 1986

This list excludes the species that have disappeared from Morocco or whose occurrence is not currently documented well enough.

Insectivora
- Algerian Hedgehog   (Erinaceus algirus)
- Desert Hedgehog   (Paraechinus aethiopicus)
- North African Lesser White-toothed Shrew   (Crocidura whitakeri)
- Tarfaya's Shrew   (Crocidura tarfayaensis)
- Greater White-toothed Shrew   (Crocidura russula)
-                 (Crocidura lusitania)
-                 (Crocidura bolivari)
- Pigmy White-toothed Shrew   (Suncus etruscus)

Macroscelidea
- North African Elephant Shrew   (Elephantulus rozeti)

Chiroptera
- Larger Rat-tailed Bat   (Rhinopoma microphyllum)
- Lesser Rat-tailed Bat   (Rhinopoma hardwickei)
- Egyptian Slit-faced Bat   (Nycteris thebaica)
- Greater Horseshoe Bat   (Rhinolophus ferrumequinum)
- Lesser Horseshoe Bat   (Rhinolophus hipposideros)
- Mediterranean Horseshoe Bat   (Rhinolophus euryale)
- Mehely's Horseshoe Bat   (Rhinolophus mehely)
- Blasius's Horseshoe Bat   (Rhinolophus blasii)
- Sundevall's African Leaf-nosed Bat   (Hipposideros caffer)
- Trident Leaf-nosed Bat   (Asellia tridens)
- Whiskered Bat   (Myotis mystacinus)
- Geoffroy's Bat   (Myotis emarginatus)
- Natterer's Bat   (Myotis nattereri)
- Long-fingered Bat   (Myotis capaccinii)
- Lesser Mouse-eared Bat   (Myotis blythi)
- Common Pipistrelle   (Pipistrellus pipistrellus)
- Kuhl's Pipistrelle   (Pipistrellus kuhli)
- Savi's Pipistrelle   (Pipistrellus savii)
- Ruppell's Bat   (Pipistrellus rueppelli)
- Greater Noctule   (Nyctalus lasiopterus)
- Serotine   (Eptesicus serotinus)
- Hemprich's Long-eared Bat   (Otonycteris hemprichi)
- Barbastelle   (Barbastella barbastellus)
- Grey Long-eared Bat   (Plecotus austriacus)
- Schreiber's Bat   (Miniopterus schreibersi)
- Free-tailed Bat   (Tadarida teniotis)

Primates
- Barbary Ape   (Macaca sylvanus)

Lagomorpha
- Brown Hare   (Lepus capensis)
- Rabbit   (Oryctolagus cuniculus)

Rodentia

- ☐ Barbary Ground-squirrel (Atlantoxerus getulus)
- ☐ Geoffroy's Ground-squirrel (Xerus erythropus)
- ☐ Large North African Gerbil (Gerbillus campestris)
- ☐ Baluchistan Gerbil (Gerbillus nanus)
- ☐ Pigmy Gerbil (Gerbillus henleyi)
- ☐ Lesser Egyptian Gerbil (Gerbillus gerbillus)
- ☐ Greater Egyptian Gerbil (Gerbillus pyramidum)
- ☐ (Gerbillus hesperinus)
- ☐ (Gerbillus hoogstraali)
- ☐ (Gerbillus occiduus)
- ☐ (Gerbillus riggenbachi)
- ☐ Lesser Short-tailed Gerbil (Dipodillus simoni)
- ☐ Greater Short-tailed Gerbil (Dipodillus maghrebi)
- ☐ Fat-tailed Gerbil (Pachyuromys duprasi)
- ☐ Shaw's Jird (Meriones shawi)
- ☐ Lybian Jird (Meriones libycus)
- ☐ Sundevall's Jird (Meriones crassus)
- ☐ Fat Sand Rat (Psammomys obesus)
- ☐ Wood Mouse (Apodemus sylvaticus)
- ☐ Barbary Striped Mouse (Lemniscomys barbarus)
- ☐ Black Rat (Rattus rattus)
- ☐ Brown Rat (Rattus norvegicus)
- ☐ House Mouse (Mus musculus)
- ☐ Algerian Mouse (Mus spretus)
- ☐ Western Multimammate Rat (Mastomys erythroleucus)
- ☐ Spiny Mouse (Acomys cahirinus)
- ☐ Garden Dormouse (Elyomis quercinus)
- ☐ Lesser Egyptian Jerboa (Jaculus jaculus)
- ☐ Greater Egyptian Jerboa (Jaculus orientalis)
- ☐ Porcupine (Hystrix cristata)
- ☐ Gundi (Ctenodactylus gundi)
- ☐ Thomas's Gundi (Ctenodactylus vali)

Carnivora

- ☐ Jackal (Canis aureus)
- ☐ Common Red Fox (Vulpes vulpes)
- ☐ Sand Fox (Vulpes rueppelli)
- ☐ Fennec (Fennecus zerda)
- ☐ Weasel (Mustela nivalis)
- ☐ Ferret (Mustela putorius furo)
- ☐ Saharan Striped-weasel (Poecilictis libyca)
- ☐ Ratel (Mellivora capensis)
- ☐ Otter (Lutra lutra)
- ☐ Genet (Genetta genetta)
- ☐ Egyptian Mongoose (Herpestes ichneumon)
- ☐ Striped Hyaena (Hyaena hyaena)
- ☐ African Wild Cat (Felis libyca)
- ☐ Sand Cat (Felis margarita)
- ☐ Caracal (Felis caracal)
- ☐ Leopard (Panthera pardus)
- ☐ Cheetah (Acinonyx jubatus)

Artiodactyla

- ☐ Wild Boar (Sus scrofa)

- ☐ Dorcas Gazelle   (Gazella dorcas)
- ☐ Edmi Gazelle   (Gazella cuvieri)
- ☐ Addra Gazelle   (Gazella dama)
- ☐ Barbary Sheep   (Ammotragus lervia)
- ☐ Red Deer   (Cervus elaphus)

SEA MAMMALS

follows Bayed and Beaubrun, 1987

Cetacea
- ☐ Sei Whale   (Balaenoptera borealis)
- ☐ Fin Whale   (Balaenoptera physalus)
- ☐ Blue Whale   (Balaenoptera musculus)
- ☐ Humpback   (Megaptera novaeangliae)
- ☐ Striped Dolphin   (Stenella coeruleoalba)
- ☐ Common Dolphin   (Delphinus delphis)
- ☐ Bottlenose Dolphin   (Tursiops truncatus)
- ☐ False Killer Whale   (Pseudorca crassidens)
- ☐ Killer Whale   (Orcinus orca)
- ☐ Risso's Dolphin   (Grampus griseus)
- ☐ Long-finned Pilot Whale   (Globicephala melaena)
- ☐ Harbour Porpoise   (Phocoena phocoena)
- ☐ Sperm Whale   (Physeter macrocephalus)
- ☐ Cuvier's Beaked Whale   (Ziphius cavirostris)
- ☐ Northern Bottlenose Whale   (Hyperoodon ampullatus)

Pinnipedia
- ☐ Mediterranean Monk Seal   (Monachus monachus)

ORCHIDS

after Raynaud, 1985

- ☐ Yellow Bee Ophrys   (Ophrys lutea)
- ☐ Sombre Bee Ophrys   (Ophrys fusca)
- ☐ Atlantic Bee Ophrys   (Ophrys atlantica)
- ☐ Moroccan Bee Ophrys   (Ophrys dyris)
- ☐ Mirror Ophrys   (Ophrys vernixia)
- ☐ Sawfly Ophrys   (Ophrys tenthredinifera)
- ☐ Moroccan Woodcock Ophrys   (Ophrys scolopax apiformis)
- ☐ Bee Ophrys   (Ophrys apifera)
- ☐ Bumble Bee Ophrys   (Ophrys bombyliflora)
- ☐ Marsh Lax-flowered Orchid   (Orchis palustris)
- ☐ Early Purple Orchid   (Orchis mascula s.l.)
- ☐ Fan-lipped Orchid   (Orchis saccata)
- ☐ Pink Butterfly Orchid   (Orchis papilionacea)
- ☐ Spitzel's Orchid   (Orchis spitzelii)
- ☐ Green-winged Orchid   (Orchis champagneuxii)
- ☐ Bug Orchid   (Orchis coriophora)
- ☐ Milky Orchid   (Orchis lactea)
- ☐ Naked Man Orchid   (Orchis italica)
- ☐ Markusi's Marsh Orchid   (Dactylorhiza markusii)
- ☐ Moorish Marsh Orchid   (Dactylorhiza maurusia)
- ☐ Robust Marsh Orchid   (Dactylorhira elata elata)
- ☐ Robust Marsh Orchid   (Dactylorhiza elata durandii)
- ☐ Tongue Orchid   (Serapias lingua)
- ☐ Small-flowered Tongue Orchid   (Serapias parviflora)
- ☐ Long-lipped Tongue Orchid   (Serapias vomeracea)
- ☐ Heart-flowered Tongue Orchid   (Serapias cordigera)
- ☐ Man Orchid   (Aceras anthropophorum)
- ☐ Giant Orchid   (Barlia robertiana)
- ☐ Lizard Orchid   (Himantoglossum hircinum)
- ☐ Pyramidal Orchid   (Anacamptis pyramidalis)
- ☐ Greater Butterfly Orchid   (Platanthera chlorantha)
- ☐ Algerian Butterfly Orchid   (Platanthera algeriensis)
- ☐ Two-leaved Scrub Orchid   (Gennaria diphylla)
- ☐ Dense-flowered Orchid   (Neotinea maculata)
- ☐ Broad-leaved Helleborine   (Epipactis helleborine)
- ☐ Red Helleborine   (Cephalantera rubra)
- ☐ Sword-leaved Helleborine   (Cephalantera longifolia)
- ☐ Violet Limodore   (Limodorum abortivum)
- ☐ Autumn Lady's Tresses   (Spiranthes spiralis)
- ☐ Summer Lady's Tresses   (Spiranthes aestivalis)

BIBLIOGRAPHY

Only some key references are listed here. For a more detailed list of ornithological publications see HEIM de BALSAC and MAYAUD (1962) and BERGIER (1987)*.

Aulagnier, S.; Thevenot, M. (1986) Catalogue des Mammifères sauvages du Maroc. Trav. Inst. Sci., Rabat, n° 41, 163pp.

Barreau, D.; Bergier, P., Lesne, L. (1987) L'avifaune de l'Oukaimeden, 2200–3600 m (Haut Atlas – Maroc). Oiseau et Revue Française d'Ornithologie 57:307–367.

Bayed, A.; Beaubrun, P. (1987) Les Mammifères marins du Maroc: inventaire préliminaire. Mammalia 51: 437–446.

Bergier, P. (1987) Les Rapaces diurnes du Maroc. Annales du CEEP, n°3, 160 pp.

Bons, J. (1967) Recherches sur la biogéographie et la biologie des Amphibiens et Reptiles du Maroc. Thèse, Univ. Montpellier, France.

Etchecopar, R. D.; Hue, F. (1964) Les Oiseaux du Nord de l'Afrique. Ed. Boubée, Paris. 606 pp.

Heim de Balsac, H. and Mayaud, N. (1962) Les oiseaux du Nord-ouest de l'Afrique. Ed. Lechevalier, Paris. 486 pp.

Heinzel, H.; Fitter, R.; Parslow, J. (1979, 4th edition) The Birds of Britain and Europe with North Africa and the Middle East. Ed. Collins, London. 336 pp.

Pineau, J.; Giraud-Audine, M. (1979) Les oiseaux de la péninsule tingitane. Trav. Inst. Sci. Rabat, série Zool. n°38. 132 pp.

Raynaud, C. (1985) Les Orchidées du Maroc. Ed. Société Française d'Orchidophilie (84 rue de Grenelle, 75007 Paris). 117 pp.

Thevenot, M.; Bergier, P.; Beaubrun, P. (1980) Compte-rendu d'ornithologie marocaine année 1979. Doc. Inst. Sci. Rabat n°5. 68 pp.

Thevenot, M.; Bergier, P.; Beaubrun, P. (1981) Compte-rendu d'ornithologie marocaine, année 1980. Doc. Inst. Sci. Rabat n°6. 95 pp.

Thevenot, M.; Bergier, P.; Beaubrun, P. (1983) Rapartition actuelle et statut des rapaces nocturnes au Maroc. Le Bièvre, 5: 27–39.

Thevenot, M.; Beaubrun, P.; Baouab, R. E.; Bergier, P. (1982) Compte-rendu d'ornithologie marocaine, année 1981. Doc. Inst. Sci. Rabat n°7. 120 pp.

*can be obtained from CEEP, BP 304, 13609 Aix en Provence, FRANCE, or from P. Bergier, 4 Avenue Folco de Baroncelli, 13210 – Saint Rémy de Provence, FRANCE. Price: 120 FF.

LOCAL CONTACTS AND SOCIETIES

There are several organisations which deal with nature conservation in Morocco. The Institut Scientifique, Charia Ibn Batouta, BP 703, RABAT-Agdal conducts research into Moroccan natural resources and its 'Zoologie and Ecologie Animale' department is responsible for ornithological activities, such as running a ringing centre (using rings of Museum National d'Histoire Naturelle de Paris, France) and a bird record committee. It has a Museum, with a bird collection and a library but its publications have been unavailable in recent years.

Scientific expeditions can obtain permits for ringing and for visiting certain areas from the Institut Scientifique or from the Division de la Chasse, Pêche et Protection de la Nature, Eaux et Forêts; Ministère de l'Agriculture et de la Réforme Agraire; RABAT-Chellah.

The universities in Rabat, Casablanca, Fès, Meknès, Agadir and Marrakech have their own zoology departments and may sometimes be able to provide bird information.

To help to improve or update this Guide, please send any comments, sightings or reports from birdwatching trips to Morocco to:

Patrick and Fédora Bergier
4 Avenue Folco de Baroncelli
13210 Saint Rémy de Provence
FRANCE

↑ AZROU

Zeida

↑

P.21

3 Km

|

∨

Track

↑

500M

↓ × X

Quarry ()

Sparse grassy area

Dupont's
Lark

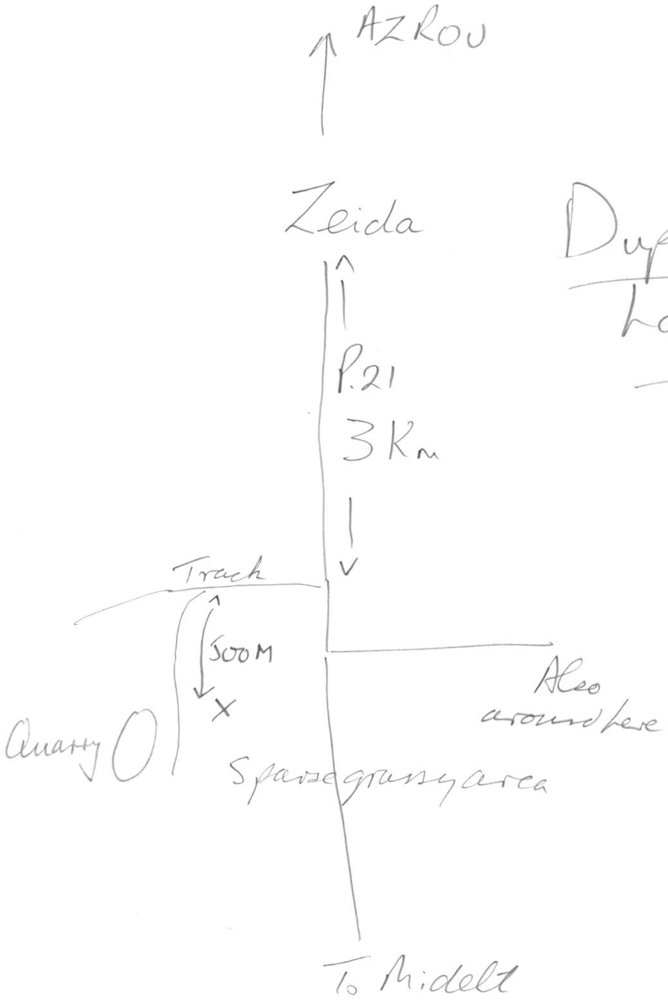

Also
around here

To Midelt

Pre dawn & 1½ hours
thereafter

BirdingWorld
Vol 3 No. 11

Dark-chanting Goshawk

To Taroudannt P.32 ——————————————— → To Aoulouz

□ Garage
(Shell)

□ IGOUDAR

Square → □

WADI

⚡ Windpump

□← —Football pitch

↑

= 3 Km

(X) HILL

Palm
Groves

(X) HILL

N / E / S / W (compass)